THE PUFFIN BOOK OF
100 EXTRAORDINARY INDIANS

THE PUFFIN BOOK OF

100

extraordinary

INDIANS

Text by VENKATESH VEDAM
Illustrations by MOHITH O.

PUFFIN BOOKS
An imprint of Penguin Random House

PUFFIN BOOKS

USA | Canada | UK | Ireland | Australia
New Zealand | India | South Africa | China | Singapore

Puffin Books is part of the Penguin Random House group of companies
whose addresses can be found at global.penguinrandomhouse.com

Published by Penguin Random House India Pvt. Ltd
4th Floor, Capital Tower 1, MG Road,
Gurugram 122 002, Haryana, India

Penguin
Random House
India

First published in Puffin Books by Penguin Random House India 2022

Text copyright © Penguin Random House India 2022
Illustrations copyright © Mohith O. 2022
Content researched and developed by excalibEr Solutions

ISBN 9780143453147

Typeset in Sabon LT Std by Manipal Technologies Limited, Manipal

Printed at Repro India Limited

www.penguin.co.in

Contents

1.	Abhijit Banerjee	1
2.	Abul Kalam Azad	5
3.	Aditi Pant	9
4.	Adar Poonawalla	12
5.	Amrita Pritam	16
6.	Amrita Sher-Gil	20
7.	Anasuya Sarabhai	24
8.	Anna Hazare	27
9.	Anshu Gupta	30
10.	Arati Saha	33
11.	Arundhati Katju	36
12.	Arunima Sinha	40
13.	Atal Bihari Vajpayee	43
14.	Avani Lekhara	47
15.	Ayyankali	50
16.	Bhaichung Bhutia	54
17.	Barkha Dutt	58
18.	Bhagat Singh	62
19.	Bhimsen Joshi	66
20.	Bhupen Hazarika	69
21.	Bimal Roy	72
22.	Bina Das	76
23.	Ustad Bismillah Khan	80

24.	Byju Raveendran	83
25.	Charles Mark Correa	86
26.	Chhatrapati Shivaji Maharaj	90
27.	Cornelia Sorabji	93
28.	Daya Bai	96
29.	Deepa Malik	99
30.	Devi Shetty	102
31.	Dadasaheb Phalke	106
32.	Dhyan Chand	109
33.	Dilip Kumar	113
34.	Dutee Chand	116
35.	Faqir Chand Kohli	120
36.	Gaidinliu	123
37.	Ganga Bhishen Agarwal	126
38.	Gauhar Jaan	129
39.	Gauri Sawant	133
40.	Geeta Dharmarajan	137
41.	Gulzar	141
42.	Guru Dutt	145
43.	Guru Nanak	148
44.	Ileana Citaristi	152
45.	Indra Nooyi	155
46.	Irom Sharmila	158
47.	Ismat Chughtai	161
48.	Jagadish Chandra Bose	165
49.	James Douglas Tytler	169
50.	Jayalalithaa Jayaram	172
51.	Jhalkari Bai	175

52.	Kailasavadivoo Sivan	178
53.	Kailash Satyarthi	181
54.	Kamal Haasan	185
55.	Karsanbhai Patel	188
56.	Kasturba Gandhi	191
57.	Kishore Kumar	195
58.	Krishnadevaraya	198
59.	Lal Bahadur Shastri	201
60.	Lal Ded	204
61.	Laxmi Narayan Tripathi	207
62.	Mah Laqa Bai	210
63.	Mahashay Dharampal Gulati	213
64.	Mahasweta Devi	217
65.	Mahesh Bhupathi	220
66.	Manmohan Singh	223
67.	Manvendra Singh Gohil	226
68.	Mangte Chungneijang Mary Kom	229
69.	Mira Nair	233
70.	Mukesh Ambani	237
71.	Mulk Raj Anand	241
72.	Nain Singh Rawat	245
73.	Naina Lal Kidwai	249
74.	Nandini Harinath	253
75.	Narain Karthikeyan	256
76.	Panini	260
77.	Prakash Padukone	263
78.	Prasanta Chandra Mahalanobis	266
79.	Priyanka Chopra	270

80. Purnima Devi Barman   274
81. Raghuram Rajan   277
82. Ramnath Goenka   281
83. Romila Thapar   284
84. Romulus Whitaker   287
85. Rukhmabai Raut   290
86. Rukmini Devi Arundale   293
87. Sam Manekshaw   297
88. Satya Nadella   300
89. Satyendra Nath Bose   303
90. Savitribai Phule   307
91. Smita Patil   310
92. Sonam Wangchuk   314
93. Srinivasa Ramanujan   317
94. Sundar Pichai   321
95. Suryakant Tripathi 'Nirala'   324
96. Sushmita Sen   327
97. Tarla Dalal   330
98. Vikas Khanna   333
99. Virat Kohli   336
100. Zubin Mehta   340

Genius Economist

Name: Abhijit Banerjee
Birth Date: 21 February 1961
Place: Mumbai, India

Little Jhima walked back home after another dull day at South Point School, Kolkata (previously Calcutta). As he neared his house on Mahanirban Road, he noticed that his neighbourhood friends were still playing. While he'd been cramming lessons in school, his friends would have had a whale of a time roaming on the streets and playing all sorts of exciting games. Oh, what a life they had! Jhima envied his friends sometimes.

Playing hours were restricted by what was left of the day post school and homework—no wonder his friends could beat him at any sport! Maa and Baba explained that his friends were children from poor families and could not go to school. Jhima had the privilege to attend school. His parents' house was near one of the biggest slums of Kolkata and hence, Jhima's friends were all children from the slum, with lives that were vastly different from his own.

The exposure to the poor so early in his childhood stayed with Jhima, who grew up to be known as Abhijit Banerjee, the world-famous economist.

He strived to understand how the lives of the poor could be different, something that no economic theory ever dwelt on. His work (along with his wife Esther Duflo) brought him the ultimate laurel in the form of the Nobel Prize for Economics in 2019. In their own words, the hardworking couple wanted to 'stop reducing the poor to cartoon characters and take the time to really understand their lives, in all their complexity and richness'.

Abhijit always wanted to study mathematics, and therefore joined the famous Indian Statistical Institute in Kolkata as an undergrad. However, not happy with the 'heavy' environment around studying mathematics, he shifted to economics.

Later, in one of his interviews, he talked about the importance of fun in one's life and work: 'I try to arrange my day so that it is at least one or two hours when I am doing something that I'm genuinely enjoying . . . I love cooking so I cook almost every day . . . I like playing racket sports so I usually arrange my day to either play tennis or ping pong or badminton . . .'

Young Abhijit was highly influenced by his teachers and his parents, who were also professors of economics. While his father, Dipak Banerjee, taught at Presidency College, his mother, Nirmala Banerjee, lectured at the

Centre for Studies in Social Sciences, Kolkata. Abhijit also taught at Harvard University after earning his own PhD from the same place.

Currently, he is the Ford Foundation International Professor of Economics at the Massachusetts Institute of Technology. He believes in conducting 'field experiments' to understand and work on the fractured economy across the world. For example, his team experimented with the idea of providing remedial tutoring and teaching assistants to students with special needs at selected schools in Mumbai (previously Bombay) and Vadodara. The result was noteworthy. The learning capabilities of these children showed progress within a few days. This system is now deployed in more than a lakh Indian schools.

Abhijit, along with his wife, Esther Duflo, also a professor at MIT, travelled through many villages and towns across the world to find information and collect data for their research on poverty. This allowed them to find that there is not much difference in how the poor and the rich want to lead their lives. They share the same desires and are equally rational. The couple believes that well-targeted help can uplift the poor. However, it isn't easy to find the area that needs focus in each individual's life.

Abhijit sees himself continuing his work for the upliftment of the poor. 'I enjoy very much what I am doing, I think that this might open some more doors, give us a chance to do some more useful interventions or study some more useful interventions, make the case that these things actually matter. Maybe people will listen to us a little bit more as a result of the prize.'

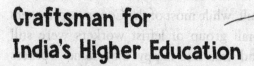

Craftsman for India's Higher Education

Name: Abul Kalam Azad
Birth Date: 11 November 1888
Place: Mecca, Saudi Arabia
Death Date: 22 February 1958
Place: New Delhi, India

Shortly after the end of World War II in 1945, Lord Wavell, the British viceroy of India, announced that general elections would be held in the country. Azad was the president of the Congress Party at that time and had interacted with Wavell earlier. Upon hearing the election announcement, he thought the British government had no reason to keep thousands of Indian political prisoners in jail. He wrote to Lord Wavell requesting general amnesty (the act of an authority by which pardon is granted to a large group of individuals) in the interest of the government as well as the Indian people.

The argument was that since the government's intention in holding the general elections was to create a new political atmosphere, they might as well release the political prisoners. Wavell agreed with Azad's views and gave release orders but did not announce a general amnesty. As a result, while most of the Congress prisoners were freed, a small group of leftist workers were still behind bars. Azad was not happy that some workers were still in jail as he saw no difference between them and the freed ones as their participation in anti-British activities was the same.

Subsequently, he wrote another detailed letter to Wavell in which he said that not freeing all political prisoners would be unfortunate for India and that Wavell should agree to release everyone by granting general amnesty. This time the viceroy agreed and the remaining Congress workers were also freed—such was the respect that Azad commanded. He was regarded as a person with high moral integrity and an intellectual son of the soil by one and all.

Sayyid Ghulam Muhiyuddin Ahmed bin Khairuddin Al Hussaini, later known as Maulana Abul Kalam Azad, was born in present-day Mecca. His father was a scholar and it is said that Abul learnt English without his father's knowledge, for he wanted Abul to get only traditional Islamic education. By his late teens, Abul had realized that his true passion was journalism. As a result, in his early twenties, he started a weekly

Urdu newspaper called *Al-Hilal* (The Crescent). Young Azad (his pen name), much influenced by Mahatma Gandhi, later joined the Indian National Congress and became involved in several movements like Khilafat movement, Satyagraha, Dandi March and the Quit India movement. Like many other freedom fighters of those days, he was sent to prison several times. He was one of the members who tried to convince the British that a free India would embrace both Hindus and Muslims, strongly opposing the Partition between India and Pakistan. He was quite vocal in his criticism of Congress and Jinnah when they agreed to the Partition.

Post-Independence, Maulana Abul Kalam Azad served as the first education minister in the Indian government from 1947 until his death in 1958. During his tenure, he actively promoted free and compulsory universal education till the age of fourteen, along with secondary and vocational training. He was an advocate for female literacy and said, 'No program of national education can be appropriate if it does not give full consideration to the education and advancement of one-half of the society that is the women.'

He was a visionary, and a promoter of both science and culture. Indian educational structure saw great development and it is under his governance that the first Indian Institute of Technology (IIT), the Indian Institute of Science, Jamia Millia Islamia in Delhi, School of Planning and Architecture and University Grants Commission

(UGC) were established. He also introduced cultural academics by setting up the Sangeet Natak Akademi, Lalit Kala Akademi, Sahitya Akademi and the Indian Council for Cultural Relations. He believed 'educationists should build the capacities of the spirit of inquiry, creativity, entrepreneurial and moral leadership among students and become their role model.'

The Indian government posthumously granted Maulana Abul Kalam Azad the Bharat Ratna in 1992. Several major institutions in India have been named after him. His birthday, which falls on 11 November, is celebrated as National Education Day.

Pioneer Oceanographer

Name: Aditi Pant
Birth Date: 5 July 1943

As young Aditi neared the end of her experimental work for her PhD in Physiology in Marine Algae from Westfield College, London, during 1971–72, she had a pressing question—what now?

And fate had the answer for her.

During the last leg of her programme, she met Professor N.K. Panikkar, a senior Indian scientist, the founder and director of the National Institute of Oceanography (NIO), Goa. Speaking to him, a lot of questions came up in Aditi's mind, and one was whether India had jobs in oceanography. Professor Panikkar challenged, 'All I know is that there is a lot of work waiting for the person who has the guts to take it up. Of course, you will get far better salaries just about anywhere else.' Aditi took up this challenge. She dropped her plan to continue

9

abroad, joined NIO and relocated to India in 1973 after completing her doctorate.

Aditi Pant then went on to create history by becoming the first Indian woman (along with Sudipta Sengupta) to set foot on Antarctica.

According to Aditi, she was heavily influenced by her parents. Her mother taught her the importance of consistency early in life. She would say as she cooked—it was all about consistency. And while her mother taught her to pay attention, her father taught her to question everything. Talking about 'why and how things happen' was part of everyday dinner conversation. Growing up, she enjoyed trekking and hiking with her father, which made her want a career that allowed freedom of movement, not only of thought.

Aditi had been excited about science since she was a child. However, when she read Sir Alister Hardy's *The Open Sea*, the life of plankton described in that book blew her away. The book nurtured her existing interest in the field and a lifelong interest for marine biology and oceanography was born. She then decided to continue her study further in marine sciences.

At NIO, Aditi covered the west coast of India with her colleagues. Many times, she was the only woman in her team. Like other team members, she spent nights sleeping on the beaches and ate at local eateries. The hard work she put in gradually led to an offer of a ten-year-long programme in the Antarctic Ocean to study the food chain.

Antarctica is every oceanographer's dream and for Aditi it had come true—a proud moment for the country. The next four months were spent on harsh icy terrain as she, along with her team, unravelled interesting information about food chains, physics, chemistry and biology in the Antarctic Ocean. Working under harsh conditions, she says, 'It's difficult to work in the cold. Your numb fingers don't obey you; you have to warm them up every now and then. Everything takes longer than usual.'

During their study, Aditi and her team were also instrumental in establishing (the now defunct) Dakshin Gangotri, the first Indian scientific research base station in Antarctica. It is now totally submerged in ice and replaced with another Indian station at a separate location. Aditi had the chance to go for a second expedition to Antarctica to further work on her research on oceanography.

After serving NIO for seventeen years, Aditi joined National Chemical Laboratory in Pune. There she continued her research on the enzymology of salt-tolerant and salt-loving microbes in the food chain.

Aditi's incredible story is an inspiration to many young girls to not only pursue a career in the not so 'well-known' field of oceanography but also to remain curious and ask questions.

The Covid Vaccine Commander

Name: Adar Poonawalla
Birth Date: 14 January 1981

The year 2020 saw the world battling the unprecedented Covid-19 pandemic that raged across the globe at a devastating pace, devouring lives and collapsing economies and livelihoods. For an emerging economy like India, the impact on the poor was especially severe. As the nation went into lockdown, the only ray of hope was from pharma companies racing against time to produce that one vaccine that could halt the virus in its path.

Despite being the world's biggest vaccine manufacturer, Serum Institute of India, headquartered in Pune, was relatively unknown outside the pharma sector till then. The young CEO, Adar Poonawalla, inherited the mantle from his father, Cyrus Poonawalla, who had established the company back in 1966. The prodigal son joined the Serum Institute in 2001 after graduating from the University of Westminster. Within a few years, he had taken the institute to the top of the charts by expanding the product base and spreading operations worldwide. As the CEO in 2011, he took the decision to acquire a global vaccine manufacturing company. Within a few years, the company doubled the number of countries to which it was exporting vaccines.

Back home, Adar launched the oral polio vaccine in 2014, which benefited crores of kids. He also became the board member of Gavi, the Vaccine Alliance, whose mission is to vaccinate children worldwide against lethal and incapacitating diseases like polio, tuberculosis, diphtheria and hepatitis B.

In March and April of the year 2020, Adar backed undertrial Covid vaccines, including AstraZeneca, Novavax and a few others. Adar decided to invest about 200 million dollars and shore up the Serum Institute facilities, including buying raw material, arranging for additional equipment and provisioning the workforce. In addition, he was able to raise about 300 million dollars with the help of the Bill & Melinda Gates Foundation. Critics perhaps thought this young CEO was crazy to have invested so much in undertrial drugs. But Adar reasoned that without committing to these trials and taking a head start in mass production, there would be no hope down the line to mass-produce enough vaccines in the coming months.

Aware of the risk that if the clinical trials for these vaccines failed, the losses would be immense, he still chose to go ahead. The gamble paid off brilliantly as the AstraZeneca vaccine, called Covishield in India, proved effective and safe for humans after multiple trials. Thanks to the proactive approach, the vaccine could ultimately be produced in mass numbers. In one of his interviews, he said, 'I've always had this sense of responsibility to India and the world because of the vaccines we were making, but never have we made a vaccine so needed in terms of saving lives.'

While the fight with Covid is far from over and even as its second wave unleashed an even bigger terror, the foresight that Adar showed helped increase the pace of vaccination and contain Covid cases within a manageable limit. Driven and enterprising Adar has wilfully shouldered an enormous responsibility.

Apart from producing vaccines in large numbers to cater to the massive global requirements, he is also involved in philanthropic activities. A year after taking the reins of the company in 2011, he founded the Villoo Poonawalla Foundation in memory of his late mother. The foundation's objective is to enhance lives through healthcare, education, sanitation and environmental conservation. A champion of an inclusive society, he believes in providing equal opportunities to the transgender community in India, 'I have always believed that healthcare and dignity should be fundamental human rights.'

Today, Adar Poonawalla is a household name in India. If India is considered the largest exporter of vaccines globally, then it is due to the efforts of Adar and his workforce at Serum Institute of India.

Rebel Poet and Writer

Name: Amrita Pritam
Birth Date: 31 August 1919
Place: Gujranwala, Pakistan
Death Date: 31 October 2005
Place: New Delhi, India

At the young age of eleven, Amrita lost her mother. During those days, her maternal grandmother handled the kitchen in their house. Amrita's father, with whom she lived, was a writer as well as an editor and hence, people of different religions used to frequent their place. One day, the little girl noticed that her grandmother had kept three glasses separate from the other vessels in the kitchen. Apparently, these glasses were used to serve tea or lassi to Amrita's father's Muslim friends. The vessels for Hindus and Sikhs were never mixed with these three glasses.

Amrita objected to this partisan treatment of Muslims, saying that, henceforth, she would drink water or tea from only the 'Muslim' glasses. Since she could not be kept thirsty, word soon reached Amrita's father, who immediately put an end to this discriminatory practice. Subsequently, no vessel in the kitchen was Hindu or Muslim. At the time, neither her grandmother nor Amrita knew that she would grow up and fall in love with a Muslim man.

This vessel incident reveals Amrita's rebellious nature. She went on to question religion and morality in her poetry and lived a life that was much ahead of her times. Today, Amrita Pritam is one of the most celebrated Punjabi writers of the twentieth century.

Amrita was a curious child whose intelligence was reflected in the difficult questions she asked people around her. Watching her mother suffer through a long illness turned her into an atheist at a very young age. She started writing after her mother's death and published her first collection of poems *Amrit Lehran* (Immortal Waves) at the age of sixteen in 1936. Her name was changed from Amrit Kaur to Amrita Pritam when she got married, in the same year.

She continued writing beautiful romantic poetry until she joined the Progressive Writers' Movement, a literary movement in which writers wrote about the happenings in society at the time. As a result, in 1944 she released an anthology titled *Lok Peed* (meaning anguish felt by people) that emphasized the socio-economic impact of the ongoing World War II and the resulting famines.

Later, during her migratory journey from Lahore to Delhi in 1947, she wrote an epochal poem portraying the chaos, terror and pathos suffered by the people at the time of Partition: *Ajj Akhaan Waris Shah Nu* (To Waris Shah), which is to date considered to be one of the most poignant works on the Partition. It also remains one of the most widely read works of modern Indian literature.

Amrita wrote in Punjabi, Hindi and Urdu. Her works oscillated between romance, feminism and society and have been translated into English, Japanese, French, Danish and many more languages. She produced several poems, short stories and novels that illustrated everything a woman wasn't allowed to be in her times—a fierce writer, an unapologetic lover and a born rebel.

Amrita chose to leave a loveless marriage in 1960— not common during those days. At the time of her death in 2005, she had been living with her partner of forty years, a writer and an artist himself, Imroz. They launched a Punjabi magazine called *Nagmani* in 1966, which gained popularity rapidly. Though it is no longer in circulation, the magazine was highly appreciated by literary writers and readers across the country.

Through her life and writings, she paved the path for herself as the first Punjabi woman writer to create her own voice in Punjabi literature—a largely male-dominated field. Amrita Pritam was the first female Indian writer to receive the national Sahitya Akademi

Award for her magnum opus, a long poem, *Sunehade* (Messages) in 1956.

A rebel with a cause who exercised her free will unabashedly, her life is an enchanting saga that could be summarized in her own words: 'Wherever the glimpse of a free spirit exists, that will be my home . . .'

Trailblazer of the Modern Movement in Indian Art

Name: Amrita Sher-Gil
Birth Date: 30 January 1913
Place: Budapest, Hungary
Death Date: 5 December 1941
Place: Lahore, Pakistan

Born to a Hungarian-Jewish mother in the early 1900s in Dunaharaszti, Hungary, this little girl would often take a fantastical journey as her mother narrated folk stories. These stories weren't new to her; she had heard them umpteen times before from her mother. However, each time she listened to the stories, the same wave of excitement that she felt upon hearing them for the first time would take over her. With each rendition, exciting images from the stories filled the girl's mind—fairies with colourful wings floating about, trees that turned red and green and blue.

The images from the stories lingered in the girl's mind long after her mother had stopped.

Every detail from the stories she heard piqued her imagination, which she then channelled into her sketchbook. She even went on to write stories and poems of her own in her sketchbook, often illustrating them. But it was drawing and colouring that became her second nature.

At five-and-a-half, much to her family's surprise, she was drawing all the time, copying her playthings like dolls and teddy bears. Unlike other children, the little girl preferred to make her own drawings and colour them; she disliked colouring in pages of a colouring book. There was little doubt that the girl was born to draw and paint.

Who would have thought that years later, this little girl with her brush would go on to become Amrita Sher-Gil, one of the most remarkable artists that the world would ever see.

Amrita's childhood was quite eventful. After her eighth birthday, Amrita's father, Umrao Singh Sher-Gil Majithia, a Jat Sikh aristocrat, shifted his family to Shimla in India, where she learnt piano and dramatics at the famous Gaiety Theatre.

In 1924, Amrita took admission in a renowned art school in Florence, Italy. After her return to India, Amrita started painting local subjects. However, it was in Paris in 1929, that the sixteen year old started her training under the famous painter, Lucien Simon, at

Académie de la Grande Chaumière and received formal training at the École des Beaux-Arts. She admired the works of European painters and started working under Lucien Simon, the French painter.

Gradually, her painting style transitioned from European to Indian. This was because she used a lot of colours in her paintings, which were more suited to the Eastern world! Taking inspiration from Mughal art and Ajanta caves, she made a foray into Indian art. She travelled through southern India and painted vignettes of life.

Some of her famous paintings include *Brahmacharis, Bride's Toilet* and *South Indian Villagers Going to Market* (collectively known as the South Indian Trilogy), as well as *Three Girls.* 'I can only paint in India. Europe belongs to Picasso, Matisse, Braque . . . India belongs only to me,' she was once heard saying. Her paintings were women-centric and inspired by the works of Rabindranath Tagore.

Amrita passed away in 1941 at the age of twenty-eight, leaving behind a gallery of magnificent paintings. While one set of Amrita's paintings depicted the unforgiving realities of rural Indians under the British rule, another set liberated the image of Indian women. She ensured her paintings portrayed her subjects with dignity.

Free-spirited Amrita Sher-Gil was one of the most remarkable Indian artists and she has been declared a 'national treasure' by the government of India. Her works are preserved in the National Gallery of Modern Art in

New Delhi. India Post released a stamp of her painting *Hill Women* in the year 1978.

Amrita Sher-Gill lived life on her own terms, often defying conventional ways of society.

First Woman Trade Union Leader

Name: Anasuya Sarabhai
Birth Date: 11 November 1885
Place: Ahmedabad, India

In the early 1900s, Anasuya—a young woman in her twenties—sat in her compound following her daily routine of combing the children's hair at the school she had established. These children were poor, belonging to different castes in Ahmedabad; she had been providing education and shelter to them.

Just then, Anasuya saw a group of fifteen mill workers walking past the road outside. She noticed that the workers seemed dazed and were walking as if in a trance. Though she did not know them well, Anasuya was concerned and asked them why they looked so pale. The workers told her that they were headed home after working for thirty-six hours (two nights and a day) without a break.

Anasuya was filled with horror upon hearing this and thought the mill workers were being exploited. Over the next few days, she learnt more about the work and lives of the mill workers. Anasuya discovered their extreme poverty and powerlessness. Mill owners and their management had been exploiting the workers by paying them low wages in return for endless work hours.

Affected deeply by their poor working conditions, her resolve to organize them and fight for their rights grew.

She got a chance to launch her crusade in 1914, when Ahmedabad was hit by a plague epidemic. Unable to sustain the burden of low wages, the mill workers requested Anasuya to take up their cause.

Thus, on the banks of River Sabarmati, a revolution began to simmer.

Anusuya took up the cudgels and addressed the gathering of mill workers. The owners of the mill were given forty-eight hours to fulfil the demands—better wages, better working conditions and fixed hours—failing which the workers would go on strike. They had to go ahead with the strike and won after twenty-one days. Mahatma Gandhi later joined the movement to voice the grievances of the mill workers.

Though Anasuya was born with a silver spoon in her mouth, to the affluent family of Sarabhai and Godavariba, tragedy struck when she lost both her parents at the age of nine. She, along with her two siblings, were raised by her paternal uncle, who married her off at the age of thirteen. It was an unsuccessful marriage and Anusuya returned to her home and became a Jain Sadhvi.

A couple of years later, she took admission in the London School of Economics with the help of her brother. She was twenty-six years old at the time. She interacted with the Fabian Society and became a participant in the suffrage movement for women's rights in the UK. The ideas of social justice and social equality influenced her.

Thus, upon her return to India in 1913, Anusuya found her true calling. She not only opened a school that granted admission to poor students irrespective of their caste but also bathed and taught them herself. Soon after, she also opened crèches, maternity homes and toilets for women.

An ardent follower of Gandhian ideologies, Anasuya was referred to as Pujya by him for her consistent work towards empowerment of the deprived. Fondly called Motaben ('elder sister' in Gujarati), Anasuya Sarabhai holds an exceptional place in history as the first woman trade union leader in India and also as the founder of Ahmedabad Textile Labour Association, India's oldest union of textile workers.

Social Activist Who Shook the Country

Name: Anna Hazare (born Kisan Baburao Hazare)
Place of Birth: Bhingar, India

The year was 1965. A man of short stature was driving an army truck carefully to Khem Karan, the India–Pakistan border. The man, Kisan, was a part of the Indian military convoy that was advancing on the mud-beaten road near Khem Karan in Punjab. As an erstwhile flower seller and a young man in his early twenties, he wasn't a natural fit in the army but had joined the emergency call for service a couple of years previously, when the Indian army was looking to shore up its numbers.

As he manoeuvred the truck outside Khem Karan, little did Kisan know that the day would be a turning point in his life. The truck reverberated with the war cries of army men, followed by a few seconds of enemy aerial fire. And then came the silence of martyrs in the truck. The only survivor was the driver, Kisan, who had miraculously escaped with a minor wound on the forehead.

Remembering the incident years later, he remarked, 'That incident sent me thinking. I felt that God wanted me to stay alive for some reason. I was reborn in the battlefield of Khem Karan. And I decided to dedicate my new life to serving people.'

Kisan, or Anna Hazare, as he came to be known, made the world a better place through movements aimed at promoting rural development, increasing government transparency and eliminating corruption in public life.

Anna Hazare's childhood was not comfortable. He studied till middle school and had to forgo further education due to shortage of funds. He started selling flowers, and since he was very hardworking, he became the owner of two flower shops in a short time. He then joined the Indian Army in the year 1960, where he learnt life's valuable lessons. After a little more than a decade of serving in the army, he returned to his village, which was in a poor state, both economically and environmentally.

Education and employment rates were at their lowest and crime and alcoholism were rampant. In this scenario, following Vivekananda's direction of 'calling to the youth', Anna formed Tarun Mandal (Youth Association). The youth idolized his principles and worked tirelessly towards prohibiting social evils like smoking, drinking, domestic violence and many more causes. Anna also encouraged people to form grain banks, watershed embankments and charitable trusts.

Anna led many anti-corruption movements, including one related to the Right to Information (RTI) Act. 'Introducing amendments like controlling the appointment of information commissioners will only lead to a dictatorship. I am at a loss to fathom why the RTI amendments were introduced and passed in the Lok Sabha,' Anna said. He said that the RTI Act granted power to the citizens and therefore it should not be amended.

However, his most famous movement was the one concerning the Jan Lokpal Bill. He wanted to hold the government accountable for its actions and as a result, suppress corruption. He declared a Satyagraha movement for the bill and sat on an indefinite hunger strike. Many prominent people of civil society supported him. He banned politicians from meeting him during the strike and called it 'the second struggle of independence'. Finally, the government bowed to his demands, and he ended his fast after ninety-eight hours. The whole episode gained a lot of media attention and Anna became a household name.

Anna Hazare earned a Padma Shri and a Padma Bhushan from the President of India in 1990 and 1992 respectively.

The Clothing Man

Name: Anshu Gupta
Place of Birth: Meerut, India

On a cold day in December in the early 1990s, a young journalist was scanning the streets of Delhi for an interesting story. When he saw a middle-aged man gingerly pushing a cart with his 'wares' hidden beneath white shrouds occupying the full length of the cart, he asked the man out of curiosity, 'What do you sell?'

The man stopped the cart and stared at the journalist. 'Read this, sahib,' he said, pointing at the verbiage on the side of the cart. It read *'laawaris laash uthane wala'*. The man, Habib, picked up unclaimed corpses for a living and was employed by the police. His work involved picking up the bodies of homeless and unidentified people who had died alone on the streets or in hospitals. Each such body fetched Habib a meagre amount of Rs 20. Winters were a busy period for him because more people died due to inadequate clothing.

In another incident, the young journalist found a destitute six-year-old girl who hugged dead bodies in a cremation ground whenever she felt cold.

This shook him.

These incidents, as well as subsequent interactions with other underprivileged people in Uttarkashi (where hundreds of people died and innumerable people lost their homes after the earthquake in 1991) had a profound impact on this young journalist, Anshu Gupta.

He saw the inadequate clothing of poor people as a metaphor for other hapless situations that the underprivileged suffer from—including scantiness of food and shelter. These interactions had sown the seeds of the non-profit Goonj—a Delhi-based non-governmental organization founded by Anshu in 1999, along with his wife Meenakshi.

In just under two decades, Anshu became a pioneer in the field of social entrepreneurship. His 'Cloth for Work' (CFW) and 'Not Just a Piece of Cloth' (NJPC) campaigns led to significant changes in the lives of numerous people. While CFW provides people with clothing, NJPC makes sanitary napkins for poor women from reusable pieces of cloth collected from households. The idea is to give clothes to charity in a dignified manner and spread the importance of health and hygiene.

These two initiatives earned him the sobriquet of 'The Clothing Man'.

Over the years, Goonj has helped bring about a paradigm shift in the way charity is done in India. Instead of indulging in just giveaways, Goonj has encouraged 'mindful' giving. It has also empowered communities and individuals by providing them with the means to solve their problems. People are encouraged to work and are rewarded with clothes and other material.

Interestingly, Anshu's reporting journey began when he was still in school. After a road accident which confined him to bed for many months, he found solace in reading and writing articles. Those months introduced him to his journalistic abilities. He worked in the corporate sector for some time before establishing Goonj.

He is a social entrepreneur who has been motivating youth to participate in social causes and take action for the upliftment of the downtrodden. A recipient of several awards for his innovation and leadership in the social sector, Anshu is a powerful and inspiring speaker and declares, 'Goonj doesn't want to grow only as an organization; it wants to grow as an idea . . . where organizations and individuals across the world take up the work, learning from our experience and help reach the basics of life to people who need it urgently. Mindful of their dignity and their needs, not as charity.'

Groundbreaking Swimmer

Name: Arati Saha
Birth Date: 24 September 1940
Place: Kolkata, India
Death Date: 23 August 1994
Place: Kolkata, India

Arati Saha had started off as a swimming prodigy, winning her first competition at the age of five. She had gone on to win several state-level competitions subsequently and had also represented India at the 1952 Helsinki Olympics, even before she turned twelve. But the date she looked forward to was 27 August 1959, when she would attempt to enter the record books as the first Asian woman to cross the English Channel between Cap Gris-Nez in France and Sandgate in England, a 42-mile (about 67 km) stretch. Considered equivalent to climbing Mount Everest, this feat was a test of endurance that was believed to have claimed the lives of at least eight swimmers over the years.

Having worked hard for over a year for the event, Arati looked forward to the big day. However, she had a bad start as her pilot boat was delayed and she started late by forty minutes. A late start meant she had missed favourable weather and was just five miles from the English coast. Arati struggled hard and had to give up, as suggested by her pilot. But Arati was made of sterner stuff. She trained even harder and returned a month later to take up the same challenge on 29 September. Though she had to brave a rough sea with hostile waves and threatening currents, sixteen hours and twenty minutes later she entered the corridors of history as the first Asian woman to cross the mighty English Channel. After reaching Sandgate, Arati hoisted the Indian flag. This event brought new possibilities for women across India as swimmers.

Arati was born in Kolkata in 1940 into a middle-class family. She lost her mother in infancy and was brought up by her father, who worked in the army, and her grandmother. She would often accompany her father to the riverbank and enjoyed swimming there. Seeing her keen interest, her father had her join a swimming club where Sachin Nag, India's first Asian Games gold medallist, observed her skill.

Nag then took her under his wing and at the age of five, Arati won the first medal of her swimming career.

Within the span of the next six years, she won twenty-two state-level competitions in various swimming events. She set a national record in the 100m breaststroke in 1951. The following year, she represented India at the Helsinki Olympics. She was the youngest member of the team. Brojen Das, another Indian who had crossed the English Channel, recommended Arati's name for the same feat in 1958. Arati did India proud by not only crossing it but also finishing it fourth-fastest. This earned her a Padma Shri the following year, making her the first Indian female sportsperson to be granted this award. Later, Arati completed her studies and worked in railways.

Arati Saha died at the age of fifty-four due to an illness. However, her story of determination, success and resilience continues to inspire many even today.

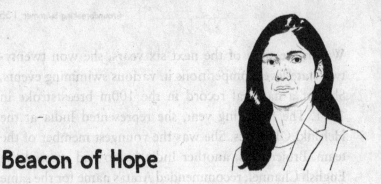

Beacon of Hope

Name: Arundhati Katju
Birth Date: 19 August 1982
Place: Prayagraj, India

In 2013, the LGBTQIA+ community in India faced a significant setback as the Supreme Court reinstated the outdated legacy of the British colonization of India— Section 377 of the Indian Penal Code that criminalizes romantic relationships between consenting adults of the same gender, punishable by law. The Supreme Court had overturned the Delhi High Court's 2009 visionary judgement that decriminalized Section 377.

Arundhati Katju was a public-interest litigator arguing for the LGBTQIA+ community along with her team of lawyers. This was not only a professional battle for her and her partner Menaka Guruswamy but a personal one too, since they were also fighting the judgement as proud members of the LGBTQIA+ community. And so, all was not lost yet; it would be a long journey but they were hopeful.

In one of the hearings, the judge had asked the government lawyer if he had ever known an LGBTQIA+ person; the lawyer had replied in the negative. So, when Arundhati and her team of lawyers went back to court in 2016 to oppose Section 377, they brought influential LGBTQIA+ Indians from diverse backgrounds who had shown up to share their stories of discrimination and suffering.

Arundhati and her team of lawyers also represented young LGBTQIA+ students from the IITs to speak about the existing repercussions of Section 377 they were living with. The young petitioners voiced their aspiration to be recognized as equal citizens of India without being treated like criminals. Arundhati and her co-lawyer Menaka Guruswamy argued convincingly that life deserves to be different for these individuals. The court's decision was momentous when it announced that LGBTQIA+ people can no longer be criminalized and are fully protected under the constitution. As CJI Dipak Misra said, 'Certain sections of our society have been living in shackles of exclusion. We have to vanquish prejudice and embrace inclusion and ensure equal rights.' One of the judges added that history owes an apology to LGBTQIA+ people and their families.

The judgement day was 6 September 2018, which went down as a major milestone in India's journey towards becoming an equitable society.

Arundhati studied law at the National Law School of India University, Bengaluru (previously Bangalore) and then further at Columbia University, New York. She mainly fights civil litigation cases and cases that are of public interest. Her uncle Markandey Katju is a former Supreme Court judge and was perhaps an inspiration to her.

Some of her other cases that caught the limelight are the AgustaWestland bribery case (middlemen and officials allegedly received kickbacks in a deal to purchase helicopters for VVIPs), the 2G spectrum corruption case (UPA government allegedly sold 2G spectrum licenses on conditions favourable to certain telecom operators) and the Jessica Lal murder case (model and celebrity barmaid Jessica Lal was shot dead during a party). Arundhati has fought around a hundred cases pro bono (professional work undertaken voluntarily and without payment). However, her most notable case was fighting for the rights of the LGBTQIA+ community.

In 2019, her name was included in *TIME* magazine's 100 Most Influential People. On being asked that while the law has changed will the society also change, her answer was, 'Society changes because LGBT people are changing and gaining the confidence to live the lives they dreamt of. I look forward, in the coming years, to seeing LGBT people from every walk of life in positions of leadership—from government and business, to academia, media and the judiciary.'

While there is still a long way for India to go and hopefully new paths are paved for the judicial system to allow LGBTQIA+ Indians their right to formally marry people they want to and actively practice equality, there's no denying that it's lawyers like Arundhati who ensured that India took the first step in that direction.

Fearless Mountaineer

Name: Arunima Sinha
Birth Date: 20 July 1989
Place: Lucknow, India

12 April 2011

After receiving an employment call for the post of head constable from CISF (Central Industrial Security Force), eager and energetic, twenty-one-year-old Arunima boarded the Delhi-bound Padmavati Express at Lucknow. As usual, the compartment was full, but somehow, she managed to squeeze into a corner seat as the train gathered speed.

Arunima sat pondering over her future, gazing out into the darkness of the night, when someone tugged at the gold chain around her neck. Seeing a young girl travelling alone, some goons tried to rob her while the other passengers watched silently. Arunima, a national-level volleyball player, tried to fight back and reclaim her chain from the goons.

The angered miscreants teamed up and threw her out of the running train. Arunima's body hit another train rushing past on the adjacent track and fell. When she tried getting up after the two trains had passed, she realized that one of her legs was dangling tenuously from the thigh and the other one had protruding broken bones; blood spurted non-stop.

The train had run over her left leg.

Her mind was still active, though her body was brutally battered. She screamed for help, but the only thing that turned up in the darkness was some rodents. It was only by dawn that nearby villagers spotted her and rushed her to a hospital. To save her life, the doctors had to amputate her left leg below the knee.

She turned around what could have been a setback for her with her indomitable spirit. Not only did she claim the ground that was beneath her with a prosthetic leg but also the highest point in the world—Mount Everest. Arunima Sinha became the first female amputee to scale Mount Everest.

Born to an army man and a healthcare professional based in Lucknow, Uttar Pradesh, she is the middle child of three. Growing up, she loved sports and is a former seven-time national volleyball player. She also loved football and hockey. She was often called *ghamanja khiladi* (meaning 'all-rounder') by many.

Driven to join the paramilitary forces, she applied to CISF at the suggestion of her brother-in-law. It was on the same journey to the interview that Arunima lost her leg but found the biggest goal of her life.

Post recovery, Arunima joined a mountaineering course at Nehru Institute of Mountaineering, Uttarkashi. She also trained at the Tata Steel Adventure Foundation under Bachendri Pal, the first Indian woman to conquer Everest. With the help of funds arranged by various institutions and individuals, she completed her climb to the summit in fifty-two days on 21 May 2013.

There was no looking back once she started climbing.

Today, Arunima has successfully conquered several peaks: Everest in Asia, Aconcagua in Argentina, Elbrus in Europe, Kilimanjaro in Africa, Kosciuszko in Australia, Carstensz Pyramid (Puncak Jaya) in Indonesia. Her most recent climb was the majestic Mount Vinson in Antarctica in 2019.

Arunima has been conferred with many awards and accolades, including the Padma Shri in 2015 and the Tenzing Norgay National Adventure Award. She has also been featured as one of the 'People of the Year' in the 27th edition (2016) of the *Limca Book of Records*.

'The mountains we climb are not made only of rock and ice, but also dreams and desire.
The mountains we climb, are mountains of the mind.'—*Mountain* (2017)

Arunima is a force of nature and her story is reflected in these lines. She hopes to one day destroy the stereotypes associated with disability. Her vision is to set up a free sports academy for the poor and disabled.

Gentleman Statesman

Name: Atal Bihari Vajpayee
Birth Date: 25 December 1924
Place: Gwalior, India
Death Date: 16 August 2018
Place: New Delhi, India

On 24 September 1965, the staff inside the Chinese embassy in New Delhi were taken aback at the sight of 800 sheep in front of the gate. When they looked closely, they saw that some of the sheep even had placards around their necks that read: 'Eat me but save the world!'

It emerged that the mastermind behind this peaceful and good-humoured protest was a young politician by the name of Atal Bihari Vajpayee from the Indian opposition party—Jan Sangh.

Vajpayee, known for his wit and sharp mind, had found this novel way of protesting against China's repeated threats to start a war with India over a case of 800 sheep and 59 yaks at the Sino-Indian border in Sikkim. China had alleged in August that year that livestock had been stolen by Indian troops from the Tibetan herdsmen close to the Sikkim border. While a seemingly insignificant event in the context of the strained relationship between the two nations, the allegation by China had surprisingly dragged on, with the two countries exchanging diplomatic blows. Vajpayee had come up with this high-hearted protest as a practical answer to China's threats of another war.

Nearly four decades later, Vajpayee is recognized as the most revered Indian PM of all time. During his tenure as the prime minister of India, he visited China in 2003, paving the way to reopen the trade route with China through Sikkim.

Atal Bihari Vajpayee was born to Krishna Devi and Krishna Bihari Vajpayee on 25 December 1924. His parents followed the Sanatan Dharma and believed in education, high moral values and culture. His grandfather was a Sanskrit scholar who could easily insert shlokas in casual conversations, and his father was a poet and a teacher. It was natural for Atal to be interested in literature and poetry since he was exposed to it at an early age.

Atal Bihari Vajpayee is known as one of the greatest orators and debaters the country has produced. Even today, he is remembered by his speeches that are loved by the masses.

After finishing his post-graduation, he had started studying law but quit midway as India got its freedom and the nation was enveloped in changing times.

Atal joined the RSS (Rashtriya Swayamsevak Sangh) at the age of fourteen, where he enjoyed intellectual discourses and disciplined exercise regimes. He was highly influenced by Narayanrao Tarte, a *swayamsevak* who explained to him the complex fabric of the RSS. In 1942, at the age of seventeen, Atal was influenced by the Quit India movement. He was arrested and kept in Agra's jail for twenty-three days. He was released after it was ruled that he was one of the peaceful protesters. However, this incident haunted him throughout his life.

Atal believed in Gandhiji's socialism and positive secularism. After jumping into politics, he was inspired by Jawaharlal Nehru, Jayaprakash Narayan, Morarji Desai, Deendayal Upadhyaya and Syama Prasad Mukherjee, whom he had assisted on Kashmir affairs in his early days in politics.

Vajpayee's biggest contribution is the Golden Quadrilateral or GQ, the country's first nationwide project to build a network of four-lane highways connecting the four big cities of India (Delhi, Kolkata, Mumbai and Chennai). After assuming charge as the prime minister in 1999, GQ was his first dream project and is recognized as the biggest infrastructure intervention in the roadways sector in post-independent India.

Considered to be one of the heroes of Indian politics, he was liked equally by his own party members and opposition members. He was multifaceted—not just a powerhouse of respectable politics but also a former journalist, a writer and a poet. He loved good literature, food and music.

He was conferred the Padma Vibhushan by the Congress-led Narasimha Rao government in 1992 and the Bharat Ratna in 2015. His legacy lives on in the form of his poems even after his death:

Why shouldn't I live every moment to the fullest?
Why shouldn't I admire the beauty in every fragment?

The Girl Who Never Gave Up

Name: Avani Lekhara
Birth Date: 8 November 2001
Place: Jaipur, India

Life had been cruel to Avani; a car accident at the tender age of ten while travelling with family had paralyzed her below the waist. In the months and years following the accident, she had been confined to her home and was rather withdrawn. At the range, the young girl first tried her hand at archery, but it was too hard. Next, she went for shooting, something that would change Avani's life forever. She tried the 10-metre rifle. Though she had difficulty holding the rifle, with some help, she was able to shoot ten shots, all of which landed inside the black circle.

Okay, we can try shooting, she thought.

Six years later, Avani had won a gold medal at the 2020 Tokyo Paralympics. In doing so, she won a billion hearts and became a beacon of hope to all those overwhelmed by the obstacles in front of them.

Avani was born to a middle-class family in Rajasthan, and she initially viewed the accident and her immobility as some kind of nightmare that would soon pass on. However, the truth sank in slowly when she remained bedridden for six months. Initially, even sitting up was a challenge as she couldn't balance herself. But then she accepted her situation, understanding that it was not in her control, and decided to focus on her life ahead. She joined school and made friends and then she discovered shooting.

Initially, shooting was just a pastime during vacations, but her father encouraged her to pursue it, wanting to cheer up his daughter. Soon, Avani began winning competitions at school and later on at the state level. A turning point in her journey was reading the autobiography of champion shooter Abhinav Bindra, India's only Olympic gold medallist prior to the 2020 games. The book, *A Shot at History*, motivated her to aim high. 'I want to become the first female sportsperson to win a gold medal for India at the Paralympics,' she vowed to herself.

With relentless focus, courage and a positive attitude, Avani achieved her goal on 30 August 2021, winning an individual goal in the women's 10m air rifle and setting a new Paralympic world record. Avani had won her first international medal at the 2017 World Shooting Para Sport (WSPS) World Cup in Bangkok and had followed it up with silver medals in the UAE and Croatia in the subsequent years before hitting the bull's eye in Tokyo.

Shooting is an expensive sport. When Avani played her first match, she did not have gloves or a kit and even borrowed a rifle. However, noticing her talent, soon the Sports Authority of India, GoSports Foundation and Paralympic Committee of India (PCI) came forward to provide her with the necessary support and improve her game further.

To come out with flying colours at the international level requires rigorous practice and dedication. In the case of Avani, the Covid-19 lockdown before the Paralympics meant that her coaches and physiotherapists were not available. However, an indomitable spirit ensured that she practised shooting within her house by installing an electronic target. Coaching, physical and mental trainings were all online and taken through the phone.

Avani is also studying law and dreams of being a judge, apart from winning laurels for India in shooting. She says, 'Life consists not in holding good cards, but in playing those cards you hold well.'

Resilient Social Reformer

Name: Ayyankali
Birth Date: 28 August 1863
Place: Venganoor, India
Death Date: 18 June 1941
Place: Tamil Nadu, India

Ayyankali was born into the Pulaya caste, which was considered untouchable and discriminated against by the existing archaic caste system. Amongst other things, Dalits of the time were prohibited from dressing like the upper castes, accessing public roads and riding in animal-driven carts. The discrimination included being derided as 'untouchables'. But instead of accepting the injustice that had continued for generations, he decided to take up the reins as an anti-caste social reformer and defy every known norm of this inhumane social structure.

In 1893, at the age of thirty, Ayyankali decided to challenge these unconscionable caste codes. He dressed in white with a turban, like a member of the powerful Nair community and rode a new *villuvandi* (bullock cart) on a public road. The Nair community was enraged at this defiance and tried to stop the crusader at several places during the journey and there were clashes, but he didn't back down.

Ayyankali's bullock-cart activism became a significant milestone in the history of the Dalit movement in Kerala. On another occasion, he walked as part of a rally for asserting the rights of Dalits in Balaramapuram, which came to be known as the 'walk for freedom'. An 'upper-caste' mob attacked the rally and a fight ensued—the riot came to be known as the Chaliyar riots. Ayyankali continued protesting and defying convention and working on making Kerala an equitable society throughout his life.

Today, he is revered as one of the most influential Dalit leaders of Kerala.

Ayyankali was born in Kerala, described as the 'madhouse of caste system' by Vivekananda. This was because the Hindu caste system prevalent in Kerala at the time had 500 divisions and subdivisions. The system emerged with the agrarian society, where the lowest caste tilled the fields and the landlords belonged to the highest caste.

Since Ayyankali's parents worked in fields, they belonged to one of the lowest castes. While his family was financially better off than other families, he still had to face the atrocities from the caste oligarchs. Fearless in nature, he questioned the decrees of those times, and even formed a group of like-minded people, giving rise to Dalit activism. The group would assemble in the evenings after work and sing and dance to protest against the discriminatory society. This earned him the titles of Urpillai and Moothapullai.

Later, he encouraged more Dalit men and women to join his fight against discrimination, even providing martial arts training. The group came to be known as the Ayyankali Pada (*pada* meaning 'army'). Ayyankali believed in education for all, irrespective of caste and that only education had the power to shake the foundations of the prevalent caste system.

However, access to education for all was against the norms of those times. Despite fighting for the cause, and even after violent clashes between the Pulayas and the Nairs, when Ayyankali did not succeed, he organized the first-ever strike of labourers working in fields owned by the upper castes. It was only in 1910, and after government intervention, when Ayyankali's vision of education for all without any discrimination was fulfilled.

After being appointed as a member of the Assembly of Travancore (known as the Sree Moolam Popular

Assembly, i.e., SMPA, or Praja Sabha), he played an important role in establishing community courts.

Kerala, one of the most progressive states of India, owes a great deal of its transformation to Ayyankali, who worked relentlessly against the archaic caste system and helped the region become a more liberal and inclusive society.

The Torchbearer of Indian Football

Name: Bhaichung Bhutia
Birth Date: 15 December 1976
Place: Tinkitam, India

October 1987 during the Cricket World Cup in the Indian subcontinent.

The school's audio-visual room was bursting with loud cheers as the students and their sports teacher watched a thrilling cricket match between Zimbabwe and New Zealand. Dave Houghton's batting heroics had nearly brought victory to Zimbabwe when Martin Crowe ran backwards and pulled off an impossible-looking catch. It sealed the match for New Zealand.

The teacher yelled, 'Great catch!'

'Sir, what is so great about the catch?' asked an eleven-year-old boy, adding that he could easily make a similar catch. The teacher dismissed the boy's confidence and explained the difficulty associated with the catch. He then reminded the boy that a footballer wouldn't know the nuances of cricket. However, the boy stood his ground and accepted the challenge to make a catch similar to Crowe.

The following morning, the teacher found the boy in the field with his friends, willing to prove his point. The teacher hit a shot similar to the way it was done in the match they'd watched the previous day. The boy ran backwards just like Crowe and caught it. The teacher repeated, this time sending the ball flying even farther. Same result, the boy caught it again. Stunned by the boy's abilities, the teacher realized that little Agya wasn't just another aspiring footballer.

Agya would grow up to be one of the most successful and talented sportsmen. He soon shot to fame as Bhaichung Bhutia, the torchbearer of Indian football in the international arena.

Ugen Sangey, later known as Bhaichung, was born to fieldworkers Sonam Topden Bhutia and Dorji Doma Bhutia in Tinkitam, a small town in Sikkim.

From an early age, Bhaichung showed exceptional football dribbling skills. At ten, he won himself a scholarship from the Sports Authority of India, which helped him get admission in a well-known public school in Gangtok. There, he shone brightly on the field. Bhaichung considers Manas Chakraborty, his football coach at school, his greatest motivator.

Coming from a family of football lovers, Bhaichung was introduced to football at a very early age. All their conversations would either begin with the sport or eventually turn to it. He and his family would religiously play the game every weekend. It was during these games that Bhaichung finessed his skills.

Initially, Bhaichung's parents were sceptical about his interest in making a career in football. However, they were convinced by his mentor Karma Bhutia. He had Bhaichung join the Boys Club at thirteen. Within a few years, hard work and determination propelled Bhaichung into the world of mainstream football. From inter-school competitions to national-level competitions and international seasons, his growth was steady and consistent. He made his debut in international football in 1995 at the Nehru Cup, held in Thailand. Bhutia scored for India against Uzbekistan in the same tournament and became India's youngest-ever goalscorer at nineteen.

Over the course of his football career, he made 104 appearances and scored forty goals. He hung up his boots in 2011.

Bhaichung now owns a chain of Bhaichung Bhutia Football Schools (BBFS), with academies spread across India. He believes that no talented Indian kid should be deprived of good coaching facilities due to a lack of money or other resources.

He also founded the Indian Football Foundation (IFF), which is one of the first not-for-profit organizations for budding football players belonging to economically weaker sections of society.

'I feel it is my duty to undertake this responsibility to bring a fundamental change and ensure the young talent is nurtured in the best possible manner. Indian Football Foundation is a step in this direction—as it will provide those opportunities to the most talented players irrespective of their socio-economic background.'

I.M. Vijayan, three-time Indian Player of the Year, described Bhutia as 'God's gift to Indian football'. Bhaichung has been honoured with many awards, including the Arjuna Award (1998), Padma Shri (2008) and Asian Football Hall of Fame (2014). He continues to remain an inspiration for every kid who is confident they can make a goal or copy Martin Crowe's impossible-looking catch.

Daredevil Journalist

Name: Barkha Dutt
Birth Date: 18 December 1971
Place: New Delhi, India

In 1999, during the Kargil War, the Indian Army had taken positions on the highway with their heavy artillery targeting the peaks of Tiger Hill, which Pakistan had illegally occupied along with several other areas of Indian territory. As expected, there was retaliation from the other side, who also had the advantage of height.

Amidst this, a young journalist in her mid-twenties who had been working in journalism for only a couple of years had taken the road less travelled to cover the war for which she had to convince her employer, NDTV, as well as the Indian Army. As Barkha watched in horror from the highway, bombs rained down, engulfing everything in a thick blanket of black smoke, sending people scampering around. The car she and the cameraman had used to travel from Ladakh to Kargil was shelled and the scared driver escaped, taking her personal belongings and clothes. Barkha and the cameraman found themselves closeted in the bunker along with fifteen army men. The atmosphere outside the bunker would have scared the bravest and Barkha was no exception.

However, she displaced her fear by focusing on survival and telling a televised war story in India from ground zero—something that had never happened before. Since there was no live broadcasting, all the footage was shot on tape and she was handing them over to army officers making trips to Delhi, which were then handed over at the studio.

Barkha considers her experience at Kargil a masterclass in not only journalism but also life.

Witnessing heart-wrenching reality, Barkha learnt the true meaning of courage when she learnt to continue doing her job even after realizing that the Indian soldiers she was seeing and reporting on may never make it back. Her coverage of the war brought an example of authentic and trustworthy journalism to Indians. However, there were those who criticized the live broadcasting of her commentary, for giving away critical locations. They argued that a more careful approach should have been taken.

However, Barkha's will to travel to a dangerous place, overcome fear, experience the adrenalin rush and bring the story back to the audience at the cost of her own safety brought a breed of journalism that had never been seen before in the country. She inspired a generation of youngsters to believe in the power of authentic and sensitive journalism and to pursue a career in it.

More than two decades after Kargil, she felt the same responsibility when she reported from the ground during India's Covid-19 crisis, bringing to the fore many untold stories that shed light on the actual devastation caused by the pandemic, especially the exodus of migrant workers. Reporting for over eighty days non-stop, she leapt into lorries and trains to travel with migrant workers rushing back to their native places. She visited the sick in hospitals and interviewed people on the road. 'There was no way I was going to understand the magnitude of what's happening unless I got out and I told the story from out there,' said the courageous reporter in one of her interviews. Such is her dedication towards her work.

Being the daughter of Prabha Dutt, who was also a famous journalist, Barkha has journalism in her blood. She is a true reflection of her mother, as could be gauged from her quote, 'My mother's appetite for adventure, her dogged pursuit of the story, her rejection of anything that sought to constrict her, and her determination to be her own person even when it made her unpopular, would remain the deepest influences on my own life.'

Barkha jumped into journalism immediately after completing her master's degree in mass communication. She worked with a television news channel for twenty-one years before quitting it to start her own venture while also continuing to write opinion columns in the national and international dailies.

Whether it is live reporting from places where natural disasters have struck or ground reporting of conflicts in Kashmir, Pakistan, Egypt, Libya, Iraq or Afghanistan, Barkha has been a fearless reporter.

For feisty Barkha, 'praise and criticism are two sides of the same coin' and she wears both lightly.

The Revolutionary

Name: Bhagat Singh
Birth Date: 27 September 1907
Place: Lyallpur (pre-Independence India)
Death Date: 23 March 1931
Place: Lahore (pre-Independence India)

It was Baisakhi in the year 1919. Young Bhagat entered the quadrangular park near the Golden Temple in Amritsar with a heavy heart. He had headed there straight from school that day while his family worried about where he had gone. The young Sikh boy stood at the entrance of the park, his eyes welling up with tears as they swept the ground, coming to rest on a well in the far corner. The bodies had been cleared, but the ghost of the massacre, that had happened only a few hours ago, still lingered in the bloodstained mud, the shreds of clothes and bullets that littered the place.

A peaceful, unarmed crowd had gathered at Jallianwala Bagh to protest the arrests of prominent Indian leaders, when British troops under General Reginald Dyer opened fire, killing hundreds of innocent Indians. What was once a recreation ground for many was now a grim reminder of a ghastly act.

The boy took an empty bottle from his pocket and knelt down. He saw his hands tremble as he scooped up the mud and filled the bottle. Later at home, when he finally spoke, he showed the bottle to his mother and said, '*Biji*, this mud is our people, it has their blood. I will not let their sacrifice go waste.' Bhagat kept the bottle of mud on a rack and prayed to it daily, often offering flowers.

It was this visit to Jallianwala Bagh that ignited the spark of freedom in Bhagat Singh.

Bhagat Singh was born in 1907 in the village of Banga in Punjab (now in modern-day Pakistan) to Kishan Singh, who was a member of the Ghadar Party—a movement to overthrow British rule in India— and Vidyavati Kaur, who was later called Punjab Matha due to the sacrifice made by her son. Bhagat Singh had four brothers and three sisters, all of whom fought for the freedom of the nation.

Raised in a patriotic family, Bhagat Singh's patriotism was visible even when he was in school. Initially, Bhagat was influenced by Gandhiji and joined his non-cooperation movement. However, the movement was called off after a clash between the police and the protesters. Many people were killed and it is remembered as the Chauri Chaura incident.

After this, the young nationalist believed that armed conflict was the only way to attain freedom from the British Raj. He, along with his accomplices Rajguru and Sukhdev, became the revolutionary trio that the British started dreading.

In 1928, the Simon Commission was set up to keep an eye on political activity in India, but it did not have a single Indian representative. A large protest was held where James Scott, the police chief, killed Lala Lajpat Rai, a revered writer and politician. Bhagat Singh and his comrades hatched a conspiracy to kill the British police officer. Instead, they allegedly killed junior officer J.P. Saunders in a case of mistaken identity.

Later, Bhagat Singh, along with Batukeshwar Dutt, threw two bombs into the Central Legislative Assembly while a session was going on. The bombs were non-lethal, harmless and the idea was 'to make the deaf hear'. This act was a protest against the passing of two repressive bills.

He vocally protested the British rule and later popularized the slogan 'Inquilab Zindabad' (Long live the revolution).

Already under the scanner, Bhagat, Rajguru and Sukhdev were sentenced to death and hanged on 23 March 1931. Bhagat Singh was twenty-three years old at the time.

From that day onwards, the martyr is referred to as 'Shaheed' Bhagat Singh. India observes their execution day as Shaheed Diwas. Not just a nationalist, Bhagat Singh was a socialist too. He believed in equal opportunities, gender equality and social justice. He penned enormous political and social writings on burning issues like caste, communalism, language and politics.

As India's greatest revolutionary, Bhagat Singh's legend will continue to be told for countless generations to come. His words, 'They may kill me, but they cannot kill my ideas. They can crush my body, but they will not be able to crush my spirit' will remain etched in history.

Classical Music Maestro

Name: Bhimsen Joshi
Birth Date: 4 February 1922
Place: Gadag, India
Death Date: 24 January 2011
Place: Pune, India

Back in 1991, Pandit Bhimsen Joshi was at a hotel in Bengaluru for a concert. He was already a legend in Indian classical music and was famous across the length and breadth of the country.

A day before the concert, a gentleman met him in his hotel room and said, 'I have heard you sing really well. I know your concert is tomorrow, but can you come to my home tonight and perform for my guests?' He then offered to pay a couple of lakhs.

Panditji was livid after hearing this. Turning to another musician who happened to be with him, Panditji said in Kannada, 'Get this man out of my room.' Such was

Bhimsen Joshi's respect and love for his music. He would never sell his music in this way.

No matter how big the temptation, he had a strong willpower as far as his music was concerned. And perhaps it was this hidden willpower that also gave him extraordinary stamina to overcome challenges. As the story goes, a bad cold on the day of the concert risked his performance later that day. Panditji asked the organizer for fifteen green chillies. Eating the chillies made him sneeze and forced water out of his eyes and nose. In a few minutes, his cold had disappeared and he was ready for the concert.

Bhimsen Joshi probably inherited his love for music from his paternal grandfather, who was also a musician. However, it was his mother who influenced him with her ability to sing bhajans beautifully. Early in childhood, when he was as young as three, he would wander off to listen to the adhan (prayer) emanating from mosque loudspeakers or to listen to bhajans at temples. It is said that he left home at the age of eleven after a petty quarrel with his mother over some ghee-rice.

The young lad sang songs in trains and buses to earn money and moved between various cities before landing in Kundgol, Karnataka. His musical journey took a clear direction as he learnt music from Sawai Gandharva. He shared a robust relationship with his master. In one of his interviews, he said, 'What one learns from one's guru has to be supplemented by individual genius, or else one will not have anything worthwhile to say. In fact, a good disciple should not be a second-rate imitator, but a first-rate improvement of his teacher.' Later, Panditji initiated the Sawai Gandharva Sangeet Mahotsav in memory of his guru. It is a music festival held annually in Pune since 1953.

Though Panditji belonged to the Kirana gharana of Hindustani classical music, he was fearless where music was concerned. He always explored, practised, experimented and played with ragas. He had a distinct singing style and was a great admirer of Mallikarjun Mansur, Ustad Amir Khan and Kesarbai Kerkar. Some of his popular ragas include Shuddha Kalyan, Bhimpalasi, Darbari, Malkauns, Abhogi, Asavari Todi and Ramkali. His rendition of 'Mile Sur Mera Tumhara' in 1988 made him popular even with those who never listened to classical music.

Bhimsen Joshi travelled all around the world and made Indian classical music famous in many countries. He was awarded the Bharat Ratna, India's highest civilian honour, in 2009.

The Bard of Brahmaputra

Name: Bhupen Hazarika
Birth Date: 8 September 1926
Place: Sadiya, India
Death Date: 5 November 2011
Place: Mumbai, India

Bhupen Hazarika and his associates were about to pack up after their onstage performance at the Ramlila Ground in Delhi, when a man approached them with a small piece of paper. It was a request for Bhupenda to play one of his iconic Assamese songs, 'Moi eti jajabor' (I Am a Wanderer). This was definitely not the first time Bhupenda was getting a request to play a song in this manner. By the late nineties, he was already well-known as the musical genius from Assam whose songs had touched hearts beyond his home state.

However, this song request was special because it had come from none other than Atal Bihari Vajpayee, who himself was a big fan of Bhupenda! Once the show ended, Vajpayee met Bhupenda and said he was waiting for the song while seated in the front row. 'I was dying to hear that song, so I sent the request,' he said. Vajpayee would introduce Bhupenda as a BJP candidate from Guwahati for the Lok Sabha elections at a packed rally a few years later. Bhupen Hazarika did not win the election. However, it took nothing away from this colossus who used music as an instrument of social change.

At ten, Bhupen sang a Borgeet (the traditional Assamese devotional song) at a public function. A noted Assamese playwright and film-maker, Jyoti Prasad Agarwala, who was in the audience, noticed him and made him record his first song a year later. By the age of twelve, he was singing songs for Assamese movies. And a year later, teenage Bhupen was composing his own songs. Simultaneously, he finished his schooling and master's degree. He worked at All India Radio for a short period before winning a scholarship to Columbia University, where he earned a PhD in mass communication. While in New York, he continued to compose songs and was awarded a gold medallion by Eleanor Roosevelt for being the best interpreter of India's folk songs.

During his early years, his voice gained a baritone that provided a distinct identity to his singing. His songs captured several emotions and themes—love, humanity, social issues, national integration and universal brotherhood—and often presented an optimistic tone. The perfect combination of beautiful lyrics and a voice that touched the very souls of listeners gained him mass popularity. Not only did he become an established lyricist, singer and songwriter but he was also a successful producer-director of documentaries and films. He even managed to convince Lata Mangeshkar, one of the greatest singers, to sing for his first directorial film.

Bhupen wrote his songs and lyrics in Assamese but sang in multiple languages. He collaborated with Kalpana Lajmi, a noted director, in 1971 and delivered many Hindi songs for films like *Rudaali* and *Daman*. The songs reflected social activism and ruled the charts for a long time.

On an international level, Bhupen gained popularity as the great Indian ballad singer whose concerts could pull huge crowds. His music is recognized as the catalyst that put folk music from north-east India on the world map. Through his music, he also interpreted Assam's rich folk heritage. During the tough days of language riots and ethnic conflicts in Assam, Bhupen Hazarika's songs evoked nationalism.

For his contributions to the music industry, he received many awards over the years. It is believed that half a million people attended his funeral, such was the popularity of the man who was affectionately called Xudha Kontho (the nectar-throated one).

The Doyen of Indian Cinema

Name: Bimal Roy
Birth Date: 12 July 1909
Place: Suapur (present-day Bangladesh)
Death Date: 8 January 1966
Place: Mumbai, India

Tapan Sinha was directing one of his Bengali movies, *Kshudhita Pashan*, at New Theatres studio in Kolkata, in 1960. And one day, over the course of shooting, he had a visitor on the set—the legendary cinematographer and director Bimal Roy.

Tapan Sinha was trying to shoot a sequence in which the arches in the background were important features within the frame and the shoot was being done by mounting the camera on a crane and moving it up and down. Despite retakes, the effect that Tapan wanted was missing and none in his team were satisfied with the shot.

Bimal Roy, who was intently watching the shooting, walked up to Tapan and asked, 'What is the exact height of the crane?' Tapan said that the crane was 13 ft high. Bimal Roy asked him to lower the crane to a height of about 10 ft, move it backwards by 3 ft, and further advised the light men to add other lights in the background. The shot then turned out exactly as desired. Tapan Sinha was impressed by the fact that Bimal Roy perceived the entire sequence without once climbing the crane or even looking through the camera—a testimony to Bimal Roy's immense technical knowledge and mastery over the craft of cinema.

Bimal Roy's strength lay in his experience as a cameraman, which further added to his skill set as a director. Each frame in his films stood out for its photography. In all his works, he took great care to reveal the light source. During those days, the source of light was not paid attention to and with Bimal Roy's films came a new way of storytelling. His realistic portrayal of human beings without showing them as 'heroic' was appreciated. In addition to his technical prowess, Bimalda respected writers and their creativity. He was against making changes to original stories to make them more appealing to the box office. Thematically, he brought issues like economic inequality and social oppression to his films.

Little is known about Bimal Roy's early life. His ancestors were landowners in Suapur, now in Bangladesh.

Bimal Roy is believed to have led a simple lifestyle. Though he was in the film industry, he kept his personal life away from the limelight. He found joy in seemingly mundane things, such as plucking vegetables from the kitchen garden early in the morning. Fresh flowers always adorned his house, and so did beautiful landscapes. He was a nature lover, and this reflected in his work. It is said that many episodes from his life and immediate environment found place in his films.

It is believed that in the late 1940s, Bimal Roy pulled Bengali cinema out of the abyss. However, due to uncertain times in Kolkata, he moved to the Mumbai film industry in 1950 with his family and four assistants— Hrishikesh Mukherjee, Paul Mahendra, Nazir Hussain and Nabendu Ghosh. Suddenly, an established director in Kolkata was now a migrant artist in Mumbai.

This uprooting reflected in his iconic films, too like *Do Bigha Zameen* and *Parineeta*. These two movies paved Bimalda's path to Bimal Roy Studios. Their making and release coincided with the first International Film Festival in India in Mumbai and the first Filmfare Awards. *Do Bigha Zameen* received international accolades too. In fact, it became India's official entry into the Cannes, Moscow, Peking and Venice film festivals. Later, Bimalda produced a string of iconic movies, such as *Madhumati*, *Biraj Bahu*, *Sujata*, *Bandini* and many more. Iconic storytellers like Satyajit Ray and Mrinal Sen looked up to him. While speaking of *Do Bigha Zamin*, Satyajit Ray said, 'It is a film that still reverberates in the minds of those who saw it—and it remains one of the landmarks of Indian cinema. He was thus undoubtedly a pioneer.'

Bimal Roy is known to have brought everyday ordinariness of Indian life to the big screen and most of all, his films remained true to the times they were made in. The winner of many awards, including National Film Awards and Cannes International Award, passed away at the age of fifty-six due to cancer. However, his legacy and unparalleled film-making still live on.

Unsung Revolutionary

Name: Bina Das
Birth Date: 24 August 1911
Place: Krishnanagar, India
Death Date: 26 December 1986
Place: Rishikesh, India

It was 6 February 1932—convocation day at the University of Kolkata. Twenty-year-old Bina Das was nervous. She had completed her degree recently, but her reason for looking forward to this day was entirely, different from her fellow students. She took a few steps along the aisle towards the dais and returned to her seat. Governor Stanley Jackson, who was addressing the degree holders, barely noticed her then.

Three minutes later, Bina got up again, determined to accomplish her mission. Bina took out the revolver from the folds of her sari as she reached the dais and fired two rapid shots at the governor. Stanley Jackson was not a personal enemy but, as the governor of Bengal, he represented a system that had kept 30 crores of her fellow Indians enslaved under British occupation. The governor evaded the shots by swaying and ducking. She was about to fire for the third time when the vice chancellor of the university, Hassan Suhrawady, leapt from the dais and overpowered her.

Nevertheless, she fired three more shots though the governor escaped unhurt. In the court, Bina pleaded guilty and was sentenced to nine years of imprisonment. She explained, 'I fired on the governor, impelled by love for my country, which is repressed. I sought only a way to death by offering myself at my country's feet and thus end my suffering. I invite the attention of all to the situation created by the measures of the government. This can upset even a frail woman like myself, brought up in all the best traditions of Indian womanhood.'

Bina's father was a Gandhian and a follower of the freedom movement. The atmosphere at home had instilled patriotism in Bina. She became a member of Chhatri Sangh (an organization that supported and aided women revolutionaries, teaching them how to charge at enemies using lathis and swords, motor driving and other such skills). Involved equally in the freedom struggle, Bina's mother and sister had even set up a place called Punya Ashram, where bombs for the freedom struggle could be smuggled, stored, sorted and distributed. At the age of seventeen, Bina had joined

Subhash Chandra Bose's revolutionary organization—Bengal Volunteer Corps.

Bina Das was often called the Agni Kanya (daughter of the fire god) of Bengal because of her fiery nature and fearlessness. Years in jail could not dampen her spirit. In fact, she revolted against the poor conditions in jail, too, with a hunger-strike that lasted seven days. Such was her intolerance towards injustice.

She joined the Congress Party after her release from jail and was a fearless activist in the Quit India movement, which resulted in another jail term of three years. Post-Independence, she turned into a social worker who fought for trade unions and workers' rights. She even refused the pension of freedom fighters from the ruling Congress government in protest against forceful transportation of refugees (as a result of the Partition in 1947) from East Bengal to other parts of India.

Her hopes for the nation to flourish post-Independence are evident in the opening lines of her memoir: 'Maybe, today we are unable to appreciate the significance of this event; but, in the course of time . . . true realisation will dawn upon those, our future progeny, who will build a golden future for our nation on the foundation of this hard-earned freedom.'

The British authorities of the University of Kolkata had denied Bina her graduation degree, in a futile attempt to penalize her for her anti-British activities. In 2012, eighty-one years later, the university posthumously awarded Das her pending Bachelor of Arts degree with second-class honours in English for the year 1931.

Missing from the mainstream narratives of the freedom struggle, it was tenacious freedom fighters like Bina who refused to settle for anything less than an independent country at a great personal cost.

Shehnai Maestro

Name: Ustad Bismillah Khan
Birth Date: 21 March 1916
Place: Dumraon, India
Death Date: 21 August 2006
Place: Varanasi, India

Ustadji had just finished yet another mesmerizing *shehnai* recital when a wealthy American gentleman, a multimillionaire, walked up to him. 'Stay back here in the US, Khan sahib,' he said, 'and teach us how to play the shehnai.' Ustadji said if he stayed back to teach, it would be for at least a couple of years and he wouldn't stay there alone. The American said he was ready to host Ustadji's extended family along with his friends—a group of about fifty people—and also offered money, a car and other conveniences. Amused, Ustadji replied, 'When out of India, I miss India and when touring within India, I miss Benares.' So, if the Americans could be kind enough to recreate Benares with its Ganga and the temples in America, Ustadji would be happy to settle down in the US. Needless to say, the gentleman didn't say anything further. Such was Ustadji's love for Benares, his hometown. Bismillah Khan and the city of Benares are considered synonymous.

Bismillah Khan was born as Qamaruddin Khan, into a family of musicians. His father, Paigambar Bux Khan, was a shehnai player and so was his grandfather, Rasool Bux Khan, who performed at Dumrao Palace. In fact, his uncle Ali Bux played shehnai at the Vishnu temple of Benares and introduced shehnai to three-year-old Bismillah. His uncle's performances entranced him. Slowly, Bismillah started playing the instrument too. He would practise around the temple of Balaji and Mangala Maiya in Benares. The banks of the holy river Ganges were his favourite spots. It is said that the sound of the flowing river inspired him to create new ragas.

His performance at the All-India Music Conference in Kolkata in 1937 gave him a big break. However, his most honourable moment was when his music echoed from the ramparts of Red Fort as India declared its independence on 15 August 1947. He had the nation enthralled with his shehnai recital of Raag. His audience included Mahatma Gandhi and Pandit Jawaharlal Nehru.

Bismillah Khan has composed music for two films, one Hindi and another Kannada, before bidding goodbye to the film industry, saying, 'I just can't come to terms with the artificiality and glamour of the film world.' Travelling to other countries always made Ustadji homesick, but the

Indian government insisted that he play at the Edinburgh International Festival. His live performances had worldwide coverage right after. He performed at Lincoln Centre Hall, at the United States of America, the International and Universal Exposition in Montreal, the Cannes Art Festival and many others. He was bestowed with the Padma Shri, Padma Bhushan, Padma Vibhushan and finally, India's highest civilian award, the Bharat Ratna.

An icon of the secular spirit of India, Bismillah Khan performed at both Hindu and Muslim ceremonies. He called himself a worshipper of Allah and Saraswati, and found joy in playing music for both equally. For Ustadji, music had no religion or caste. He famously said, 'Even if the world ends, the music will still survive. Music has no caste.'

During those days, musicians performing in temples were not greatly revered. However, Khan's extraordinary dedication to the instrument ushered listeners globally into mesmerizing music produced by shehnai. He began to be referred to as Ustad, or maestro, which is now a prefix to his name. Khan elevated the shehnai, an instrument traditionally reserved for weddings, to be seen as a classical music instrument.

When he passed away in 2006, he was buried with his shehnai under a neem tree at Fatemaan burial ground at Benares, with a twenty-one-gun salute from the Indian Army.

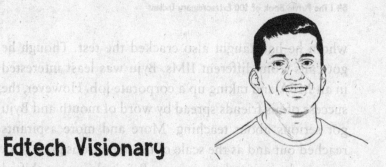

Edtech Visionary

Name: Byju Raveendran
Birth Date: 1981
Place: Kerala, India

The year was 2003. Byju was in his twenties and in India for a two-month break. He was employed as a service engineer by a multinational shipping firm in the United Kingdom. While in India, he met some of his friends in Bengaluru who were preparing for the CAT, an MBA entrance exam that allows admission to prestigious IIMs (Indian Institute of Management) across the country. Byju was from a family of teachers and was always good at maths and science at school. So when his friends asked him for help with their exam preparation, Byju did not hesitate. He simplified concepts to help his friends clear the exam. In the process, he took the exam himself, just for fun.

Byju stunned everyone with a 100 percentile score on his maiden attempt in the exam. Many of his friends whom he had taught also cracked the test. Though he got calls from different IIMs, Byju was least interested in an MBA and taking up a corporate job. However, the success of his friends spread by word of mouth and Byju got serious about teaching. More and more aspirants reached out and as the scale of his operations grew with more and more students joining, Byju's classroom shifted from a friend's terrace to an auditorium. Eventually, he quit his engineering job and took to only teaching, even travelling to other cities to reach as many students as possible.

His Eureka moment came when some of his students, who were now IIM graduates, suggested taking Byju's classes to a different level by creating content for schools. The brand, Byju's, is growing in leaps and bounds today, and is on its way to becoming the world's largest edtech company.

The journey from a village in Kerala to building a multibillion-dollar company has not been easy. Byju Raveendran comes from a humble background. He spent his childhood in Azhikode, a small village in Kerala's Kannur district. He studied in a Malayalam-medium school where both his parents were teachers. He learnt English by listening to sports commentaries on the radio.

A believer in sharing knowledge, teaching came naturally to Byju, which is why the help that he provided to his friends extended to teaching hundreds, then thousands and then millions.

In 2007, his students came up with a brand name—Byju's Classes. Byju's then launched online video-based learning for different competitive exams, with the support of a solid team. The use of technology as an enabler helped in scaling up the business. Eventually, he metamorphosed the learning experience for millions of students across India, from offline tutoring to online interactive learning. This venture grew manifold within a span of a couple of years with personalized learning experiences for every type of learner. 'Byju's—The Learning App', with its interactive videos and student-friendly format, is touted as India's most loved school learning app today. 'Our core differentiator has always been how we teach . . . to visualize and conceptualize became our strengths,' mentions Byju in one of his interviews. He believes that Byju's is teaching students how they should learn rather than what they should learn.

One of his students from the early days, Divya Gokulnath, got admission at Stanford University after his coaching. She joined Byju's later, and they got married. In 2018, Byju Raveendran won the EY Entrepreneur of the Year Award (Start-up category).

On creating an edtech unicorn, the genius says, 'The real fun is not in creating a multibillion-dollar company but in changing the way millions think and learn.'

Creator of Modern Architecture

Name: Charles Mark Correa
Birth Date: 1 September 1930
Place: Secunderabad, India
Death Date: 16 June 2015
Place: Mumbai, India

Charles Correa adored his Hornby tinplate toy train set, complete with its locomotives, wagons and a track. When he was ten, living in Secunderabad, he would spend hours in his room playing with his dear toy. When bored, he would change the tracks' layout so that the trains could run into the adjacent room or under a chair or table. Like other kids his age, he wished for more trains and tracks but it was the early 1940s and World War II was ongoing, which meant his wish couldn't be fulfilled.

So, the boy sought solace in reading the toy train catalogues he had. He would spend hours poring over the drawings and trying to recreate his own elaborate layouts on graph paper, often even while in class. His layout drawings included a variety of designs—straight rails, curved rails, sidings and crossovers. The little genius also drew trains moving through tunnels, overbridges and stations along the layout.

No, Charles did not grow up to be a railway engineer. But the elaborate railway layout drawings that he made as a child helped him understand the first architectural journal that he came across, at the age of fifteen, as he set upon his journey as a renowned contemporary architect of independent India. 'That much, I owe to Hornby,' he once said.

Charles Correa studied at the prestigious St. Xavier's College in Mumbai. Later, he went on to the University of Michigan followed by the Massachusetts Institute of Technology, where he obtained his master's degree. Missing his country, he returned to India in 1958 to launch a practice in Mumbai.

Charles Correa designed around a hundred masterpieces in India and abroad, from beautiful low-income housing to luxurious condos to iconic structures with distinct features and appearances. This included Mahatma Gandhi Sangrahalaya at Sabarmati Ashram in Ahmedabad, where he depicted Gandhiji's simple lifestyle in the buildings. He introduced 'the rooms open to the sky' (courtyards) in the National Crafts Museum in New Delhi. Other notable buildings are the Madhya Pradesh Legislative Assembly, the Jawahar Kala Kendra in Jaipur, the Hindustan Lever Pavilion in Delhi, and the Champalimaud Centre for the Unknown in Portugal.

Charles Correa was an advocate of open spaces and the outdoors. He wanted to blend 'outside with inside' while designing structures. In his essay, 'The Blessings of the Sky', Correa explained the essence behind his designs: 'In India, the sky has profoundly affected our relationship to built form, and to open space. For in a warm climate, the best place to be in the late evenings and in the early mornings, is outdoors, under the open sky. Such spaces have an infinite number of variations: one steps out of a room . . . into a verandah . . . and thence on to a terrace from which one proceeds to an open courtyard, perhaps shaded by a tree . . . or by a large pergola overhead. At each moment, subtle changes in the quality of light and ambient air generate feelings within us, feelings which are central to our beings.'

Sonmarg Apartments was his first high-rise building in Mumbai. He was also the driving force behind the planning and construction of the satellite city that came to be known as Navi Mumbai. Later, he established the Urban Design Research Institute in Mumbai in the year 1984. The main aim of the institute was to develop urban areas while protecting the precious environment. Due to his work, he was appointed as the chairman of the National Commission on Urbanization. In 2008, he accepted the post of the chairman of the Delhi Urban Art Commission.

His consistent approach was to align with the local needs while staying practical with respect to its inhabitants' requirements. The warmth in his structures reflected his pride in Indian traditions and culture.

Charles Correa was awarded the Padma Shri (1972) and the Padma Vibhushan (2006) by the Indian government. He was also commemorated with the Royal Gold Medal (Britain) and the Austrian Decoration for Science and Art.

Considered one of India's greatest architects, Charles Correa passed away on 16 June 2015, in Mumbai.

Great Warrior King

Name: Chhatrapati Shivaji Maharaj
Birth Date: 19 February 1630
Place: Shivneri Fort, India
Death Date: 3 April 1680
Place: Raigad, India

It is said that Shivaji Maharaj once stood wide-eyed in front of the Taj Mahal, a marble wonder, with his little son Sambhaji. This was mid-seventeenth century in Agra, and Shivaji had never seen a building so beautiful in his life. Running his eyes up and down the monument, he turned to his friend and guide Kunwar Ram Singh, and asked an unusual question, 'Are the foundation stones of the Taj made of marble too?'

Surprised, Ram Singh replied, 'No, they are ordinary stones.'

Shivaji sighed and said that while the beauty of the marble structure will be admired by many, the sacrifice made by the ordinary stones in the foundation will remain hidden. Similarly, as and when he would have

Swaraj (independent rule), he would be commemorated and praised, but nobody would remember the thousands of soldiers who would have laid down their lives along the way. This shows that behind the fierce warrior was a man with a tender heart who truly loved his people.

Sambhaji added that they should also build a monument like the Taj Mahal. In reply, Shivaji said that a king who ascends the throne leaves such memorials so future generations can remember him. However, a true king should also live in a manner that his life itself serves as his memorial and he shouldn't have a need to build monuments for him to be remembered.

At the time of his birth at the Shivneri Fort, Shivaji's family was going through many ups and downs. His father, Shahaji Raje, along with his brother Shambhu, had left for distant lands to serve sultans ruling the Deccan region. His mother, Jijabai, was a fearless woman who had greatly influenced his early childhood. She taught him values through religious scriptures early in life. When he was six years old, his father took both mother and son to Pune to his *jagir*. Shivaji saw the jagir being developed from scratch and it gave him first-hand knowledge of how to be an able administrator. He learnt sword fighting, *lathbaazi*, spear fighting, wrestling and archery from Dadoji Konddeo, the jagir manager.

Later, he completed his training in Bengaluru, along with his brothers. The seed of 'Swaraj' was sown as early as when he was still in his teens. The brave soldier established Maratha supremacy over substantial lands by conquering forts and territories. All the while, he maintained peaceful relations with the Mughals.

However, cracks started to appear when he started invading Mughal territories too. After his arrest in Agra by the Mughals and subsequent escape, he retaliated by recapturing his forts back in the Deccan and conquering southern provinces. Amidst all this conquering, he crowned himself the king of Maratha, acquiring the title Kshatriya Kulavantas Sinhasanadhishwar Chhatrapati Shivaji Maharaj.

A fearless combatant who led aggressive military campaigns, Chhatrapati Shivaji was known to respect all religions and promoted women's liberty. He even built a strong army and navy to secure his borders. The soldiers were skilled in various warfare techniques and martial arts. Although his death led to a decline in the Maratha glory, 400 years hence, Shivaji is recognized as one of the greatest kings that ever lived, and his life is a shining example of true valour.

India's First Female Advocate

Name: Cornelia Sorabji
Birth Date: 15 November 1866
Place: Nashik, India
Death Date: 6 July 1954
Place: London, United Kingdom

Cornelia, a little Parsi girl of about nine, lay on the floor reading a book. She was only passively listening to her mother talk to a visitor—a widowed Gujarati woman who had arrived in a cart drawn by bullocks.

It was only when the woman started sobbing as she spoke that Cornelia stopped reading and crept up to her mother's knee. Apparently, the woman had been duped into signing a blank paper. As a result, she was now penniless.

Cornelia was too young to fully understand the conversation between the woman and her mother. However, she could sense that the woman was in great anguish. Later, when her mother asked if she understood what the woman had said, Cornelia replied, 'Only that she is in great trouble and even you cannot help her.' The woman, in fact, had lost her ownership to the cunning person appointed to look after her property matters. Many Indian women in the 1870s (during the British Raj) were illiterate and suffered a similar fate by losing their properties to con men.

When Cornelia said she wanted to help such women once she grew up, her mother advised her to study 'the law' and become a lawyer in order to achieve this ambition. That day, Cornelia decided that she would do exactly that.

Thus started a long and illustrious journey chequered with many ups and downs, of the first Indian woman lawyer, Cornelia Sorabji.

Cornelia grew up in a big Parsi household with eight siblings. She didn't attend formal school. Instead, she was homeschooled by her father. She was refused admission in universities because she was a woman. However, her grit finally got her into one where she was the only girl in the college. Amidst the constant bullying by her male classmates, she excelled in studies. This enraged them further. She matriculated at the age of sixteen, topping her college in English literature.

Again, she was refused a scholarship for higher studies in England. Many prominent people of civil society fought for her right, including Sir John Kennaway (a British diplomat), Sir William Wedderburn (a member of Parliament), Mary Hobhouse (a poet), Adelaide Manning (a writer), Florence Nightingale (a famous social reformer), Benjamin Jowett (influential tutor at the University of Oxford), and others, but without any success. Not to be defeated, some of them pooled their money to send her to Oxford. Cornelia completed her law studies in the year 1892 but was awarded the degree thirty years later in 1922 as Oxford did not confer degrees on women during those times!

Upon her return, Cornelia became a lawyer for maharajas as no one else allowed her entry in formal courts. By 1899, determined Cornelia became the lawyer for women in purdah as only a woman could talk to them. She fought for their rights and dignity passionately. She even employed tutors for their children, so that the generation that followed could have better lives.

Finally, in 1904, her patience paid off when the government appointed her as the Lady Assistant of the Court of Wards to look after the properties of children under eighteen. She later became a social worker and retired from law in the year 1929. She spent her later life in London.

Cornelia Sorabji's legacy continues to live on. Celebrated as an advocate of women's rights who changed the course of history, she broke that first glass ceiling and changed the perception about women's education and even law as a profession for women.

One-Woman Army

Name: Daya Bai
Place of birth: Kerala, India

Mercy was in her teens when she followed in the footsteps of her aunts, who had joined convents in order to become nuns and dedicate their lives to the service. She left a prosperous home at Pullattu Veedu in Poovarani, near Pala in the Kottayam district, to become a missionary nun. However, on her first day in the convent, Mercy thought this was not what she wanted.

But it was during Christmas time in the Hazaribagh convent that she found her true calling. A scantily-clad group of tribals had camped near the convent. The nuns were not allowed to go out and interact with the tribals, so Mercy saw them through the convent windows. With children tied to their backs, she saw them huddled around fires in the biting cold and cooking in small utensils. Her heart went out to them and the stark contrast between the tribals and the convent atmosphere struck her. Mercy went and spoke to her trainer in the convent about wanting to go with the tribals to their village; the trainer agreed. However, the next day during Mass, she felt the same pang for tribals on her profession day (when nuns publicly profess vows of poverty, chastity and obedience). Every day, Mercy would cry in the church while training to be a nun. Seeing this, the Mother (convent head) spoke to Mercy about what she wanted. Mercy said she wanted to be part of one of the rural stations of the convent located in tribal areas.

Though not immediately, Mercy found herself in a rural station a year after that conversation. Mercy Mathew soon became Daya Bai and did yeoman work for the upliftment of countless tribals.

Following the liberation theology (emphasis on liberation of the oppressed) and holding the lives of Jesus Christ, Mahatma Gandhi and Rani Lakshmi Bai as her inspiration, Daya Bai leads a simple life in Barul village of Chhindwara district in Madhya Pradesh, amongst the Gond tribals. She practises minimalism, grows her own food on a patch of land, rears goats and chickens. She teaches tribals simple ways of leading good and respectable lives and urges them to unite against injustices of the local authorities. She says, 'The first necessity is liberation from lenders. Economic independence is the basis. Second is education. These have been my principles.'

Daya Bai visits tribals in other states and regions and uses speeches, campaigns and street plays in the local language as a medium to educate the tribals about robust agricultural activities and how to fight against unjust behaviour of moneylenders, middlemen and village chiefs.

Daya Bai has shown support to other causes too. She has travelled to different states to show her support in the Narmada Bachao Andolan (a social movement against building dams across the river Narmada, Gujarat) and the movement at Chengara (struggle for land marginalized communities and tribals in Kerala), the campaign against Endosulfan usage, also in Kerala. She has also visited villagers in Bihar, Haryana, Maharashtra, West Bengal and Bangladesh to mobilize tribals and help them know their rights.

Daya Bai established the Swayam Sahayata Group in the late 1990s. Her group's causes caught the attention of NABARD (National Bank for Agriculture and Rural Development), Gramin Bank, State Bank of India and even World Bank. The banks offered support for the upliftment of the marginalized. They also offered to open branches in local areas. This was a big step in eradicating moneylenders and middlemen who took advantage of unsuspecting and naive tribal people.

Over seventy years old, Daya Bai is a fearless warrior, a messiah fighting for the rights of marginalized tribal communities in India who crusades against many violations of social justice.

Champion Athlete

Name: Deepa Malik
Birth Date: 30 September 1970
Place: Bhainswal Kalan, Haryana

It was early June, 1999, and Deepa, an avid sports enthusiast and a part of Rajasthan's first women's cricket team, was about to receive devastating news from her doctors. An MRI had revealed that the spinal tumour, which she thought had been cured in childhood, had returned in a sinister way. They would need to operate and remove the tumour, which would paralyze her body below the chest. She was scheduled for surgery in seven days' time and beyond that, she would be in a wheelchair for the rest of her life.

So at the mere age of twenty-nine, Deepa was about to encounter a life-changing surgery. On the day of the surgery, she surprised the doctors with a request—'Instead of being taken to the operation theatre in a stretcher or a wheelchair, can I walk please? As I understand, I won't be able to walk again.' Deepa's eyes were on the stairs. As she climbed the steps, Deepa looked down and felt thankful that she had legs on that day.

The climb made her decide that she wanted to celebrate what she had even after the operation rather than be miserable about what she had lost. Three surgeries and 183 stitches may have left her paralyzed and unable to walk. But her indomitable spirit scripted one of the most unique and awe-inspiring comeback stories ever.

Deepa Malik only stood taller. She became the first Indian woman to win a medal at the Paralympic Games—a silver medal in shot-put at the 2016 Summer Rio Paralympics.

Born into an army family, she was only five years old when a spinal tumour was diagnosed, which was then treated and thought to be cured. When she was diagnosed again in 1999, she had to fight two battles at once: her second encounter with the tumour and raising two daughters single-handedly while her husband went to the Kargil War. However, Deepa, with her grit and determination, took on both.

Battling all odds, at the age of thirty-six, she decided to join sports!

Years later in an interview, she said, 'I remember when I first had the tumour all those years back, people thought I would be restricted to my house throughout my life with servants looking after my daily needs. But I wanted to break out from that mould and took to swimming, motor sports and eventually javelin and shot-put. My goal was to become independent despite my disability, and today, due to sport and the support of my family, I very much am an independent individual.'

An avid biker before the reappearance of the tumour, she revived her love for bikes. She appealed for donations to procure a customized ATV bike, which is quite expensive. She was successful at it and then left no stone unturned.

She went on to participate in many bike rallies, most on rugged terrains. Not to be limited to one activity, Deepa resumed swimming too, and participated in international events and won medals. After her silver medal at the Rio Paralympics, she won a gold medal in the 2018 Asian Para Games.

A recipient of the Padma Shri, Arjuna Award and several other medals, Deepa also holds four Limca World Records (three for motorbiking, one for swimming).

Deepa, a fearless woman, believes, 'You must take initiative and stop living on excuses. If you have a passion and if you have a dream, then you should have the courage to fulfil the dream.' Not just limited to sports, she is also a motivational speaker, an inspiration to be self-reliant and make the most out of one's life.

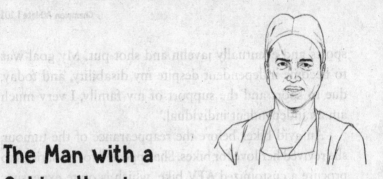

The Man with a Golden Heart

Name: Devi Shetty
Birth Date: 8 May 1953
Place: Mangalore, India

In 1967, a remarkable surgery had the entire world stumped—Dr Christiaan Barnard, a South African cardiac surgeon, performed the world's first human-to-human heart transplant operation. The medical world was enveloped by this extraordinary development, and a young boy from Karnataka, all of fourteen, was inspired. Devi decided to pursue education in medicine and become a heart surgeon. After completing his studies in Mangalore and England, he joined B.M. Birla Hospital in Kolkata as a cardiac surgeon where he performed India's first neonatal heart surgery on a nine-day-old baby.

In another episode, Devi Shetty, a young and charismatic doctor, was treating Mother Teresa for a heart attack in a hospital in Kolkata in 1984. She would often accompany Devi as he took rounds in the hospital to take stock of patients, including children with heart problems. On one of those rounds, Mother Teresa remarked, 'I know why you are here.' When the doctor asked why, she continued, 'When God created these children with heart problems, he was preoccupied and so he sent you here to treat them.'

The doctor was touched and thought it was one of the best definitions of a paediatric heart surgeon and one of the best compliments he has ever received.

Dr Devi Shetty treated Mother Teresa for the final five years of her life when her health was fragile. During this phase, he was struck by Mother's simplicity and humility. While under treatment herself, she used to visit different hospitals in Kolkata and despite being a world-renowned figure, she was polite and grounded in her interactions with people. Dr Shetty was tremendously influenced by Mother's belief that love is the most powerful weapon. Her resolve to help the underprivileged showed Dr Shetty what he needed to do—to make a difference in people's lives by providing them with affordable healthcare.

A few years later, he came to the upcoming city of Bengaluru to set up the Manipal Heart Foundation at the famous Manipal Hospitals. It is at this time that his philanthropic nature was noticed by many. He never refused to do surgery for the lack of money and took whatever his patients could afford to pay.

Dr Devi Shetty established Narayana Hrudayalaya Health City in Bengaluru in the early 2000s with the motto, 'Health for All. All for Health.' Today, it is the benchmark for affordable no-compromise healthcare in the world. Currently, the NH Group of Hospitals includes twenty-three hospitals across fourteen cities. 'India is in a phenomenal position to lead the way, make a difference and show the world a new way of delivering affordable healthcare,' said Dr Shetty in an interview.

He also conducted a lot of research and analyses on how to reduce medical costs. His endeavours allowed cardiac surgeons to perform heart surgeries at a small fraction of the cost compared to other countries in the world. This provided tremendous hope to underprivileged patients. The *Wall Street Journal* described him as the 'Henry Ford of heart surgery' as he managed to increase the number of surgeries per day at an astounding scale. (Henry Ford, an American industrialist, had benefited numerous middle-class Americans by creating the first affordable vehicle for them.)

Udaan, Dr Devi Shetty's initiative, inspires and selects deserving students and provides them guidance, coaching and support to make a career in medicine. The Narayana Hrudayalaya Foundation started a community radio programme at 90.4 wavelengths in 2017, where the conversations involve health, education, environment and culture.

Powered by the desire to help the poor, Dr Devi Shetty is one of the most respected persons in the medical fraternity that India and the world has seen. He was awarded the Padma Shri as well as the Padma Bhushan, and has performed over 15,000 heart operations.

Dr Devi Shetty continues to inspire many. His goal is to 'commission hospitals, medical facilities, and clinics across the breadth of this country, getting closer to patients and taking the promise of quality affordable healthcare to the doorstep of the country's millions.' He says, 'It is this exciting prospect that stokes my motivation to do bigger and better for the glory of the country that is mine.'

Father of Indian Cinema

Name: Dadasaheb Phalke (Dhundiraj Govind Phalke)
Birth Date: 30 April 1870
Place: Trimbak, India
Death Date: 16 February 1944
Place: Nashik, India

Dadasaheb had lined up five male actors in sarees for a particular scene in the movie *Shrikrishna Janma*. Male actors played female roles in all his films since, due to social restrictions, women in those days never got acting roles. However, this particular episode required a large number of female characters. Dadasaheb then asked all workers in the studio and any other willing amateur to wear a saree and be part of the scene! While this solved the number problem, seeing so many male faces in sarees wouldn't go down well with the audience. So Dadasaheb arranged the big group in a manner that only their backs were shown in the scene and the usual actors who did female roles would show their faces to the camera.

In another scene, a lotus was required but it was not in season. As a workaround, Dadasaheb took a big onion and cut it into the shape of a lotus; the audience did not realize the difference. Trick photography using meagre resources was Dadasaheb's speciality. In a time when no one had heard of optic lenses, he was able to take shots from different angles and leave his audience enthralled and fascinated.

It was his unstoppable efforts in the face of numerous odds when it came to film-making that laid the foundation of the Indian film industry. He is popularly known as the father of Indian cinema.

Dadasaheb, then known as Dhundiraj, had an ordinary childhood in a big family. The family shifted to Bombay (now Mumbai), when his father got a job at Wilson College, as a lecturer of Sanskrit. Dhundiraj completed his schooling in Mumbai. He was also an alumnus of Kala Bhawan, Baroda, where he learnt engineering, sculpting, painting and photography.

Always inclined towards art and creativity, prior to his entry in film industry, he worked as a photographer, a printer and a draftsman for the Archaeological Survey of India. He also assisted Raja Ravi Varma, the famous painter of Indian mythological gods and goddesses.

His biggest influence, however, came from watching the silent classic, *The Life and Passion of Christ*, which motivated him to produce India's first silent movie *Raja Harishchandra*—also remembered as India's first full-length feature film. The movie was a huge success and an astounding experience for Indians. After producing a couple of successful films, he established Hindustan Films in partnership with some businessmen, though the alliance broke after some time due to financial and creative differences.

He made movies for almost two decades, which included twenty-six short films and ninety-five full-length films. He retired after making his first film with sound, *Gangavataran*.

Even though film-making in India began in 1912, Dadasaheb's *Raja Harishchandra* was the first to be 'acted, directed and produced' by an all-Indian team. He once said proudly, 'My films are swadeshi in the sense that the capital, ownership, employees and the stories are swadeshi.'

His lifetime contribution to the Indian cinema was immortalized by the Indian government through the Dadasaheb Phalke Award in 1969. The award is annually conferred to deserving film personalities by the President of India.

The Wizard of Hockey

Name: Dhyan Chand
Birth Date: 29 August 1905
Place: Prayagraj, India
Death Date: 3 December 1979
Place: New Delhi, India

It was past sunset, and the moon was shining brightly as Subedar Bale Tiwari, who also doubled up as the sports coach for the army regiment in Jhansi, walked to the field. By then, most of the soldiers had retired to their quarters, resting and recuperating after a tough day of training.

However, Dhyan Singh was in the field, practising intensely with a hockey stick.

The young soldier had no background in hockey before joining the army, but now he seemed obsessed with the game. Dhyan had, over the past few days, quickly imbibed the tricks and techniques that Bale had taught him. Now standing near Dhyan, who had briefly paused his dribbling, Bale Tiwari said, 'Dhyan, you are shaping up so well as an individual player. But hockey is a team sport and you need to pass on the ball to your fellow players at the right time.' Dhyan nodded and said he would never forget this advice.

After practice, as he entered the quarters, Dhyan Singh was greeted by a bunch of friends. One of them remarked, 'You are out playing in the moonlight day after day. Your name should be Dhyan Chand instead of Dhyan Singh.' He smiled and moved on, but the name stuck.

The world would know the greatest hockey player ever as Dhyan Chand.

Dhyan had a happy childhood moving from one place to another as his father was in the army. He too joined the army as a sepoy when he was sixteen in 1922. It was there that he started playing hockey. Subedar Bale Tiwari saw Dhyan's interest in the sport and mentored him. Slowly, he became passionate about playing hockey. He would practise for endless hours after training. After playing many tournaments and regiment games, he was selected for the army team and went on to compete against New Zealand, where he showed his expertise in full form.

Before his selection, many believed that a lowly educated and ordinary soldier would not be given such a significant opportunity. Dhyan proved them wrong by displaying his perseverance and determination in the field and finally getting selected.

Out of twenty-one matches, the Indian hockey team won eighteen. The team struck 192 goals, 100 of which were netted by Dhyan Chand! His hard work paid off and he became a celebrity after this accomplishment.

The Indian Hockey Federation was set up in 1925, with an eye on the 1928 Olympics to be held in Amsterdam. As India was a British colony, there was much opposition from the British team to the Indian team's participation in the Olympics. However, the team received approval from the International Olympic Association.

Dhyan Chand was selected to play in the Olympic Games and the world discovered his magic. He displayed such extraordinary skill and control over the ball that, as legend has it, officials broke his hockey stick to check if there was a magnet inside. One newspaper report described it: 'This is not a game of hockey, but magic. Dhyan Chand is in fact the magician of hockey.'

What followed took Indian hockey to new levels.

Dhyan Chand played a key role in India's three consecutive gold hauls at the Olympics in 1928, 1932 and 1936. It is believed that after India's incredible win of 8–1 against host Germany, Adolf Hitler offered Dhyan Chand a post in the German army; however, Dhyan turned it down.

While he played hockey globally, he continued to serve in the Indian army. He retired after thirty-four years of service in 1956. He was conferred with the prestigious Padma Bhushan, India's third-highest civilian honour, in the same year. Dhyan Chand became a successful coach post-retirement.

Dhyan Chand's legacy is glorious. His birthday, 29 August, is celebrated as National Sports Day in India. Not just that, in 2021, the Rajiv Gandhi Khel Ratna Award, the country's highest sporting honour, was named the Major Dhyan Chand Khel Ratna Award after the legendary hockey player.

Emperor of Cinema

Name: Dilip Kumar
Birth Date: 11 December 1922
Place: Peshawar, Pakistan
Death Date: 7 July 2021
Place: Mumbai, India

Yusuf Khan, a handsome young man of about twenty, was waiting to take a local train to Dadar at Churchgate station in Bombay for a business offer to supply cots. Yusuf's family hailed from Peshawar but had later moved to Pune and then to Mumbai. He had dabbled in different businesses without much success: running a sandwich stall, selling feather pillows and of course, his family business of fruit merchantry.

As he walked up the platform to greet Dr Masani, a psychologist and a family acquaintance, Yusuf had no idea that this day would be a big turning point in his life. After learning that Yusuf was looking for a proper job, Dr Masani told him that he was going to meet the owners of the famous movie studio Mumbai Talkies. 'They may have a job for you,' he said, and suggested that Yusuf should go along with him.

Yusuf dropped his plan of going to Dadar. Instead, he took the train with Dr Masani to Malad. Soon, they were seated in the office of Devika Rani—the owner of Mumbai Talkies. Devika asked Yusuf if he knew Urdu well, to which the young man said yes, wondering what kind of a job was lined up. Dr Masani further briefed Devika on Yusuf's family background. And then, Devika asked Yusuf a question that would change his life—would he be interested in becoming an actor and joining Mumbai Talkies for a monthly salary of Rs 1250, a princely sum in those days. When Yusuf said he had no experience of acting or even watching films, Devika said, 'If you can take pains to learn about fruits and fruit cultivation, you can surely take pains to learn the craft of film-making and acting.'

What followed this conversation was the rise of a young man to be loved and known as Dilip Kumar, one of the greatest names ever to echo in the Indian film industry.

Dilip Kumar's first film was *Jwar Bhata*. He not just acted in the film but also looked at it as a tool to learn about film-making, script and screenplay writing and marketing. He believed, 'Why not think differently and take initiative to get involved with creative management of different departments of a film to ensure that a quality product was delivered?' Such was his dedication right from the beginning of his film career.

He then had a string of blockbusters year after year. In fact, his film *Aan*, India's first technicolour film, was also the first Indian film to gross around Rs 75 lakh—an unbelievable amount in 1952. With each movie, he crafted his signature style—an understated style, often mumbling his dialogues, giving each line myriad emotions and meanings. It is a style that even today is a reference point for new generations of actors. He was widely appreciated for his ability to make a character believable. Also known as the people's actor, he often represented the voice and issues of people. Having never been to an acting school, Dilip Kumar was an institution who inspired generation of actors, including Amitabh Bachchan.

With a career spanning four decades, he gave his viewers some unforgettable cinematic moments in his movies like *Mughal-e-Azam*, crowned the greatest film of Indian cinema, *Devdas*, *Madhumati* and more.

A recipient of numerous awards, including the Padma Bhushan, Dilip Kumar will be remembered as one of the greatest forefathers of the Hindi film industry to grace the silver screen.

Star Sprinter

Name: Dutee Chand
Birth Date: 3 February 1996
Place: Jajpur, India

Saraswati was upset with her younger sister, Dutee, who had been picking up empty wrappers of masala-chana cones, scavenging for leftovers. A teacher had complained to their mother. Aware of the financial limitations at home, Dutee's scavenging act was hardly a surprise for her.

Born in a family of weavers with six siblings, Dutee's family could not even spare the 10 paise required for a masala-chana cone. Saraswati had made her aware of the family's financial situation. Though just a child, Dutee understood that she had to earn money to support her family after growing up. However, at that age, as a consolation, Saraswati worked out an arrangement with an ice-cream seller to give any broken pieces of ice cream to Dutee at the end of the day for free. This meant a couple of times a week, Dutee used to get a piece of ice cream.

Since early childhood, Dutee was influenced by her elder sister. When Dutee turned six, Saraswati urged her to run every day. The sisters were born athletes.

Dutee ran races at school events and won prizes. Winning gave her a thrill and pushed her to excel in running, to which she was addicted by the time she turned twelve. When Saraswati secured a job as a constable due to her running, Dutee too decided to polish her skill to get a decent job and earn some money.

Little did she know that she was made for a bigger run! Dutee grew up and became the fastest woman runner in India.

After she took admission in a sports hostel in 2006, while the coaches saw hunger in Dutee to run, they found her body was severely malnourished. She was short and had no muscle. Still, it was her grit that pushed her to run faster than other people in the academy.

In 2010, she broke the national record, which stood at 12.21 in 100 metres at the 2010 National Juniors U-16 with her breathtaking twelve-second timing.

Dutee found her first big success on the track when she became a national champion in the under-18 category in 2012. The first Indian sprinter to reach the finals of a global athletics event—the World Youth Championships in 2013—Dutee had more to achieve and conquer.

In 2014, her dream to participate in the Commonwealth Games and Asian Games was crushed at the last moment. She was banned from competing after failing a hormone test due to a condition called hyperandrogenism—according to international regulations, her levels of testosterone were higher than the guidelines permitted for female athletes.

However, determined to run again as a competing professional athlete, she fought legal battles and the Court of Arbitration for Sport ruled in her favour. She won back her right to compete in the women's category.

Free to compete internationally again, Dutee became the first woman to represent India in three decades at the 2016 Rio Olympics. The year 2018 saw her winning two silver medals at the Asian Games.

The first Indian sports star to acknowledge being in a same-sex relationship, Dutee paved a new path for athletes from the LGBTQIA+ community to embrace their personal choices and be pitted equally as athletes.

In an interview, she said, 'I have always believed that everyone should have the freedom to love. There is no greater emotion than love and it should not be denied. The Supreme Court of India has also struck down the old law. I believe nobody has the right to judge me as an athlete because of my decision to be with who I want. It is a personal decision, which should be respected. I will continue to strive to win medals for India at international meets.'

Inspiring young athletes on the track and off it, when asked why she runs, Dutee's answer is simple, 'I don't know, but my heart tells me.' Currently, Dutee holds the women's 100-metre sprint record in India and continues to remain the winner of a billion hearts.

Father of Indian Software Industry

Name: Faqir Chand Kohli
Birth Date: 19 March 1924
Place: Peshawar, Pakistan
Death Date: 26 November 2020
Place: Mumbai, India

The phone rang and Faqir wondered who was calling him so late at night. It was a call from the customs office. Kohli was a general manager in a recently incorporated company called Tata Consultancy Services (TCS) in Mumbai, which focused on management and technology consulting.

The call was about a consignment imported for the company—a crate with a computer worth about $2500 was stuck at customs clearance. Kohli then rushed to the customs office. At the office, the customs officer took him to the crate and said that since Kohli was known and respected, they had not booked a case despite a discrepancy in the consignment; what had arrived did not match with the clearance documents provided by TCS. The officer further said he was able to see the hardware in the crate as mentioned in the document but not the software that was also mentioned in the same document! Kohli explained to the officers what software meant and got the computer consignment cleared. India had missed the industrial revolution (due to British rule) and in post-independent India, the bureaucrats knew little about invisible-to-the-eye software.

But F.C. Kohli had predicted the IT revolution in India. Popularly known as the father of the Indian IT industry, he clearly saw the glorious future for India that software would create one day, with TCS being the harbinger of the revolution.

After earning a gold medal at Panjab University, Kohli got selected in the Indian Navy. However, while waiting to be commissioned, he won a scholarship to Queen's University, Canada, where he completed his degree in electrical engineering. Post that, he did an MS at the Massachusetts Institute of Technology (MIT).

He returned to India in 1951 and thus began his extraordinary journey with Tata Group. Ambitious and optimistic, Kohli introduced digital computers for power system design and management. He then introduced mainframes in the research segment of the group. In 1969, he was brought in from Tata Electric Companies as a general manager to run Tata Consultancy Services, which later led India to become a software giant in the world. If India became synonymous with being the number one IT service provider in the world tech spectrum, it is due to the efforts of people like F.C. Kohli.

Not just a brilliant technocrat, Kohli was also known to nurture talented minds and he was not someone to be discouraged. He had implicit faith in the potential of Indian engineers, whom he had recruited from premier institutes in India and the US.

After serving TCS for decades, he retired from the post of chairman in 1996. However, his contribution to the industry did not stop. He did it all—from selecting the first faculty of IIT Kanpur to pushing for adult literacy, water purification and regional language computing efforts.

His belief, 'We are all working for the country. The profits are there, but the first step is to work and serve the people. If we do that, profits will come. Service of people means focus on client, build up your knowledge and help the client to build his clients. In the process, don't forget that I am learning as much as my client. Learning should never stop.' is a gospel for professionals to follow.

Faqir Chand Kohli was a true visionary who had unwavering belief in India's talent to defy all odds and create a new industry. Kohli's contributions to Indian IT are immense and immeasurable.

Daughter of the Hills

Name: Gaidinliu
Birth Date: 26 January 1915
Place: Nungkao, India
Death Date: 17 February 1993
Place: Longkao, India

Gaidinliu was born into a family belonging to the Zeliangrong Naga tribe. Since her village lacked schools, she never had formal education. However, she was a born leader and was hardly thirteen when she joined her cousin Jadonang's socio-religious movement, Heraka, meaning 'pure'.

Heraka had started as an initiative to reform old religious practices but went on to define a political aim for itself—to oust the British. No wonder the British saw the movement as a challenge to their reign in the north-east and executed Jadonang in August 1931 after a fake trial with an intent to quell the uprising. Little did they know that Jadonang's young cousin, Gaidinliu, would step up and take the mantle at the age of sixteen and carry forward the movement.

The young leader commanded tremendous respect from her tribe; they had in fact started revering her as an incarnation of a goddess. Under Gaidinliu's influence, the north-east version of the non-cooperation movement against the British began to spread rapidly amongst Naga tribes and household after household refused to pay taxes. Threatened by Gaidinliu's growing popularity, the British launched several campaigns to arrest her. Thanks to the local support, Gaidinliu continued evading arrest. Even informant rewards and tax holidays promised by the British did not yield any results.

While most of the resistance was non-violent, in early 1932, there was an armed conflict between Gaidinliu's supporters and the Assam Rifles contingent of the British. Later in 1932, Gaidinliu was eventually arrested in Pulomi village. After a ten-month trial, she was sentenced to life imprisonment and would be moved constantly from one jail to another in the north-east. Jawaharlal Nehru, while on a tour in Manipur in 1937, came to know about her and referred to her as a 'rani', a name that stuck ever since. It is believed that he wrote to the British requesting her release, but his request was rejected.

Later, as soon as India gained independence, Jawaharlal Nehru ordered her release in 1947, fourteen years after her imprisonment. Post her release, Rani disagreed with the Naga National Council (NNC) members who were demanding separation from India. Opposing them, she worked towards demanding a separate Zeliangrong territory within the Union of India, for which she even consolidated an army of people. This opposition didn't go well with Naga leaders, and she had to go underground in 1960.

After coming out of hiding six years later, she worked for the betterment of the people by getting them employment opportunities and working with the government for the socio-economic development of the area, for which she was awarded the Tamrapatra Freedom Fighter Award (1972), the Padma Bhushan (1982) and the Vivekananda Seva Award (1983). The government of India issued a postal stamp and a coin in her honour.

Rani Gaidinliu is a legend, an unsung hero of India's freedom movement.

Bhujia King

Name: Ganga Bhishen Agarwal
Birth Date: 1904
Place: Rajasthan, India
Death Date: 1980
Place: Rajasthan, India

Ever since Bhiki Bua introduced bhujia to her nieces and nephews during one of her visits to Bikaner in Rajasthan, twelve-year-old Haldiram (a nickname given to Ganga by his mother) was obsessed with it. From an early age, Haldiram took great interest in the kitchen and helped the ladies in the house with chopping and cleaning activities. But the process of making bhujia had captured his fascination the most.

Sitting with Bua, Haldiram practised the whole process: pouring batter into large woks using wooden ladles, skimming the oil and sieving bhujia, scooping it up and placing it on newspapers to dry. The process completely took over him, so much so that he had as many scabs as veteran snack makers in a couple of weeks because of the hot oil.

And then, one day, Haldiram had an idea.

He thought, instead of preparing the dough predominantly with besan flour, why not try moth ki dal, a lentil local to Rajasthan. To make crispier and crunchier bhujia, he used a custom mesh manufactured with much finer holes. His experiment did not end there, he even tried combinations of different spices.

Nearly a year later, Haldiram's innovation—the thinner and crispier moth bhujia—hit the markets. A snack that would take the country by storm had arrived.

At the 'old' age of eleven, Haldiram started selling bariksev bhujia. There were two reasons behind it—his love for making bhujia and his responsibility towards his family, for he was now married to Champa Devi. The snack so lovingly created by Haldiram remains popular as Haldiram's Bhujia even today.

People from all over India came to purchase Haldiram's bhujia at Bhujia Bazaar. Young Haldiram was the star of the market. Serious by nature, he was never known to joke. He was hard-working and always found ways to keep his loyal customers satisfied and happy. He not only preached quality but served quality too.

Therefore, years later, he is still known as the 'King of Bikaneri Bhujia', despite having stiff competition. However, the journey to the top was not easy.

Following disagreements between his wife and other family members, Haldiram had to leave the flourishing family business and his joint family. Not having foreseen this, he was suddenly on the street with his wife, kids and grandkids. He took it as the will of God and decided to look for a job.

Wandering one summer afternoon, Haldiram ran into his friend Allah Beli. He returned some money that Haldiram had given him a long time ago. Though the money was not enough to start a new shop, it was sufficient for Haldiram to start selling hot moong dal that his wife prepared in their meagre abode.

With a knack for marketing, Haldiram popularized his moong dal. However, his first preference was always bhujia, and after saving enough money, he rented a small shop in a temple complex where he started making and selling bhujia once more.

There was no looking back now.

Many years later, under the guidance of Haldiram, his grandsons expanded the business with manufacturing units, retail outlets and distribution all over the world. Today, the brand Haldiram is synonymous with Indian snacks.

The Gramophone Girl

Name: Gauhar Jaan
Birth Date: 26 June 1873
Place: Azamgarh, India
Death Date: 17 January 1930
Place: Mysuru, India

The Gramophone and Typewriter Limited (GTL) from London had started recording international voices on discs. To that end, Frederick William Gaisberg an agent of GTL, and his assistants were in Kolkata in 1902 in search of 'native' voices. Gaisberg visited the palaces of local zamindars and identified a famous female dancer who had a sweet voice. A makeshift studio was set up in two rooms of a hotel, where a thirty-year-old woman arrived with her relatives. Along came an entourage of musicians to play the instruments, like sarangi, harmonium and tabla.

The woman, decked out in expensive jewellery, was asked to sing as loudly as she could into a huge recording horn, the other end of which was connected to a recording machine for cutting grooves on a disc, rotating at 78 rpm.

129

Gaisberg requested the artist to sing for three minutes and announce her name at the end, since the discs would be sent to Germany for further processing and the technicians there could confirm the artist's name and label accordingly. The artist completed singing a *khayal* (a major form of Hindustani classical music) in *Raag Jogiya* and shouted out at the end, 'My name is Gauhar Jaan.' Little did she realize she would become a recording artist who went on to forever change the face of Indian classical music.

Gauhar Jaan was born as Angelina Yeoward. Her father, who was not of Indian descent, married her mother, who was also half Indian. However, her parents separated when she was quite young. Angelina and her mother moved to Benares, where they embraced Islam and renamed themselves Gauhar Jaan and Badi Malka Jaan respectively. Malka Jaan's singing and classical dance made her famous in Benares.

Soon, they shifted to Kolkata and established themselves in the court of Nawab Wajid Ali Shah, a musician and lyricist. Following in her mother's footsteps, young and talented Gauhar received training in Rabindra Sangeet, classical vocal music and Kathak. Her artistic temperament reflected in her ghazals, which she wrote under the pen name Hamdam. She performed in many royal courts and functions at various places, including Darbhanga Raj (now between India and Nepal), Kolkata, Mumbai, Bengaluru, Chennai (previously Madras), Delhi and Mysuru (previously Mysore).

After being crowned the Gramophone Girl following her first recording, Gauhar Jaan, a polyglot, recorded more than 600 songs in several languages in a span of eighteen years (1902–1920). Traditionally, a khayal is expanded into hours, however, Gauhar invented a wondrous way to consolidate an expansive form into a short time span. Though she was criticized for doing so, her unique style was later adopted by various musicians including Ustad Amjad Ali Khan (a famous sarod player).

While the famous men in Hindustani classical music were against the technological intervention in classical music, the courtesans accepted it. 'It not only helped democratize music and bring it out the from the four walls of the salons and courts, but also liberated these women artists from the clutches of their exploitative patrons,' says Vikram Sampath, author of the book *My Name Is Gauhar Jaan!: The Life and Times of a Musician*.

Gauhar Jaan, a confident musician, didn't shy away from being flamboyant, both in clothes and jewels. Over the years, while she enthralled audiences with her brilliant performances, she was also appointed as the court musician at Darbhanga Raj. She even performed at the coronation of King George V in Delhi and Krishna Raja Wadiyar of Mysuru appointed her as the palace musician. Wherever she went, she commanded respect, a virtue that women otherwise were kept away from.

Today, she is remembered as one of the forgotten artists of the past. Some scholars are now making efforts to revive her forgotten legacy. Gauhar Jaan not only challenged the authorities of the time but also married technology with Hindustani classical music—one of the ways that later helped in recording albums and archiving lost compositions.

Gauhar Jaan's captivating voice had shed a new light on the landscape of Hindustani classical music and it must be remembered across generations.

A Mother by Choice

Name: Gauri Sawant

Nine-year-old Gauri was excited for another fun-filled session of *ghar-ghar* (playing house) as she ran to join her playmates.

As a child, as soon as she had finished her homework, Gauri would run to her friends at their usual haunt in the neighbourhood, where they would be ready with pots and pans. She planned the menu on the way. *Perhaps a lavish feast to celebrate whatever occasion the girls would come up with*, she thought. Empty bottle caps jangled in her pocket; perhaps they would be handy for cutting rotis—Gauri wasn't sure. What she was sure about, however, was that she wanted to be the 'mother' and have two little doll kids to dress, feed and send to school. A pallu borrowed from one of the girls would make an ideal saree. One of her friends could play the 'father' in the scenario they chose.

Here was another thing she was sure about: Her father would *not* be happy at all to know Gauri had spent yet another evening playing with girls. But Gauri was determined not to be trapped in the gender assigned to her at birth. And her choice to live her life on her own terms made Gauri a role model not just for the transgender community in India but for all who felt they were different from the people around them.

Gauri started life as Ganesh Suresh Sawant, born to a police officer and a homemaker in Pune. At an early age, she realized she was not like the boys around her. They viewed her as a boy with effeminate characteristics. At gatherings and weddings, whenever relatives asked what Gauri wanted to be when she grew up, her answer would be: 'I want to become a mother when I grow up.'

And much later in life, after many hurdles, that is precisely what she became.

However, such public interactions embarrassed her father at the time and the situation at home became unbearable. She left home for Mumbai at the age of seventeen. She left her home and started expressing herself freely.

Gauri was born.

Gauri met a friend in Mumbai who not only gave her shelter but also introduced her to the Humsafar Trust (one of the oldest active LGBTQIA+ organizations in India). Gauri's job was to spread awareness about the importance of health and hygiene amongst sex workers. It was at that time that she transitioned and became Gauri.

During this time, Gauri was informed of a little girl named Gayatri, whose mother had been a sex worker and had died of HIV. She waged war against the girl's grandmother, who was trying to sell her. Relentless, Gauri took Gayatri home and decided to raise her. However, courts did not permit her to adopt Gayatri legally. Gayatri still called her Aai ('mother' in Marathi).

In one of her interviews, Gauri said, 'I haven't done anything for her, she's given me everything—the title of "mother", which is one of the truest manifestations of womanhood in my journey from boy to girl. On this Mother's Day, I would like to tell everyone that parenting need not be gender specific. Further, motherhood is a feeling.'

Having worked hard, Gauri then founded the Sakhi Char Chowghi Trust in 2000. The trust helps transgender people lead a meaningful and fulfilling life.

Gauri, an activist for transgender rights of marriage and adoption, was the first transgender person to file a petition in the Supreme Court for the same. The year was 2014. National Legal Services Authority (NALSA) accepted her plea and the third gender was officially recognized. This was a historic moment for transgender people across India.

The Election Commission of India appointed Gauri Sawant as one of the twelve election ambassadors from the state. In the history of elections, this was the first time that a transgender person was appointed as a goodwill ambassador in India.

Gauri's work has been replete with defying every convention and working towards a more inclusive society.

The Changemaker

Name: Geeta Dharmarajan
Birth Date: 19 September 1948
Place: Chennai, India

When she returned to India from the US in the late 1980s after working at the University of Pennsylvania, Geeta settled in Delhi. She wanted to further her writing ambitions by focusing on translations and penning books for children. However, Geeta's immediate environment brought a shift in her ambitions.

Close to her house were multiple slums, and she was drawn into providing a library for the underprivileged children by upcycling her garage. She also established a school for them in 1990 under her non-profit organization, Katha, with a magazine for children from the underserved communities. However, to her surprise, only five children joined the school when it started off. Given that the average monthly income of each family was extremely low, upon investigation, it emerged that the parents were sending kids to workshops where the children were given lunch in exchange for folding paper envelopes.

Geeta's school still remained open, and one day, a few women from the slum area walked into the school and expressed an interest in attending the ongoing activity class for children. Looking at their interest, it occurred to her that 'women can earn and children can learn'. This thought brought an income generation programme for the women to teach skills like cooking, baking, tailoring, embroidery, among others. The idea paid off, with mothers augmenting their income through these skills and allowing children to study at the school. Slowly, children from more underserved areas joined the school and carved out an unimaginably different life for themselves—thanks to the story-based learning followed in Katha schools. Concepts of languages, science, arts, mathematics, general awareness and critical thinking are taught in story form as part of this methodology, without using traditional textbooks; a child thinks, asks, discusses and acts using stories.

In over three decades of its operation, Katha has initiated multiple programmes to ensure that every child receives holistic learning and has helped over a million children out of poverty.

Stories had always been at the centre of Geeta's life since her early childhood in Chennai. She frequently visited the temples in the local area with her grandparents and keenly absorbed the mythological tales told there. Geeta's father was a doctor, whom she accompanied to nearby villages. These experiences of storytelling and service fed into her imagination. Perhaps this is why Geeta grew up believing her future was in being a storyteller for underprivileged children.

Later, as a grown up, the works of Tamil women poets from thousands of years ago influenced her thought process. She still believes that they brought forth an intense desire in her to be compassionate to all.

Geeta maintains that, at Katha, they develop stories 'not for fame, not for money but to give pleasure . . . bottom line is not profit but social change.' She is the force behind the unique Active Story-Based Learning model. This model constitutes the classroom practices module of the 'Story Pedagogy'. Along with this, Katha schools and associated organizations follow an environment-friendly curriculum. She believes that translation is a powerful tool in India. Her aim is to translate works of great composers like Kalidasa, Rahim, Kabir, Bhakti and Prakrit poets and other such great personalities, and introduce them to kids: 'I want to give children what they could forget but something that will definitely come back to them later in life. I want to help them strengthen their conscience which can tell them right from wrong.'

An inspirational writer, educationist and social entrepreneur, Geeta served as the honorary chairperson of the National Bal Bhavan in Delhi. She was honoured with the Padma Shri in 2012 for her contributions to education and literature. A true storyteller at heart, she said in an interview, 'Noam Chomsky famously said that "grammar is the building block of every language," however, I would counter that by saying that stories are the building blocks of every language! It is stories that evoke emotions and connections, and anchor us in our lives.'

The Wordsmith

Name: Gulzar
Birth Date: 18 August 1934
Place: Dina, Pakistan

Mumbai in the early sixties . . .
Legendary film-maker Bimal Roy was making his iconic film, *Bandini*. As always, Shailendra was the lyricist and S.D. Burman was the film's music director. However, a tiff between the two had resulted in Shailendra ceasing to be keen on working on the film and he persuaded his young poet friend to go and meet Bimal Roy. Gulzar, a young poet working in a motor garage to support himself, had always aspired to become a writer, though not a film lyricist.

However, he did go and meet the film-maker. Bimal Roy explained the scene to Gulzar, who penned a song that S.D. Burman liked. By the time the song was recorded, Shailendra and S.D. Burman had patched up, which meant that Shailendra was back. Seeing Gulzar's potential, Bimalda then had a conversation with the young poet, which changed the latter's life. Aware that Gulzar wasn't keen on writing lyrics, Bimal asked him to assist him on his films. He was ready to teach Gulzar the art of direction. He proposed that in case Gulzar did not like direction, he could do whatever else he liked. 'But please do not go back to that garage, that's no place for you,' he added. Gulzar accepted Bimal's offer and walked through his multifarious journey and produced innumerable gems as a lyricist, poet, author, screenwriter and film director.

The Partition between India and Pakistan in 1947 saw many families migrating from either side. Sampooran Singh Kalra, later known as Gulzar, moved to Bombay from Dina, now in Pakistan. He belonged to a hard-working Sikh family and did menial jobs in the city, including working as a painter in a car garage, to make ends meet. Always fond of literature and writing, particularly that of Rabindranath Tagore, he began writing under his pen name 'Gulzar' after his parents disapproved of his dream to become a writer.

Gulzar's life changed once he met Bimalda. His pen produced more than 800 songs, many of them masterpieces, including the popular prayer in schools 'Hum Ko Man ki Shakti Dena'; the famous 'Jungle, Jungle Baat Chali Hai' from the Hindi version of *The Jungle Book*; 'Lakdi ki Kathi'; a massive hit with every generation, 'Chaiyya Chaiyya'; the classic 'Tujhse Naraz Nahin Zindagi'; and worldwide sensation 'Jai Ho', for which he and A.R. Rahman received the Academy and Grammy Awards.

A lover of literature, Gulzar wanted to be a writer from the beginning. He joined the Progressive Writers' Association (PWA) when he was in college and doing small jobs simultaneously. It was there that he met people connected to the film industry, including Shailendra. His words, which sensitively capture the complex emotions of life, continue to touch the hearts of millions, irrespective of age and generation. He also wrote dialogues and screenplays for blockbuster films like *Maachis*, *Ijaazat*, *Angoor*, *Koshish* and *Aandhi*.

His films explored a wide array of subjects and presented characters that stayed with audiences long after the movie was over. Whether it was the sensitive take on the women in political positions in *Aandhi*, the emotional depth in his political drama *Maachis* or his attempt to explore 'grey' characters in *Ijaazat* that won him a national award, his films continue to remain a reference point for new generations.

Gulzar extends emotions through his poetry in several languages, including Urdu, Punjabi, Braj Bhasha, Khariboli, Haryanvi and Marwari. He is a natural when it comes to poetry. He says, 'The poetry is always churning in my mind, and I jot it down. I don't need any special conditions in order to produce my work. I can write anywhere, because just as life goes on all the time, this process of thinking and writing goes on alongside it.'

He has worked with the finest in the film industry, people like Bimal Roy, Hrishikesh Mukherjee, Lata Mangeshkar, Sanjeev Kumar, R.D. Burman, Asha Bhosle, A.R. Rahman, Mani Ratnam, Rahat Fateh Ali Khan and Naseeruddin Shah, to name a few. He is a recipient of several National Film Awards, Filmfare Awards, the Dadasaheb Phalke Award and the Padma Bhushan.

A lyricist, poet, author, screenwriter and film director, Gulzar continues to enthral readers, writers and his audiences with his works. He once said, 'Books taught me to read and inspired me to write.'

Ace Actor–Director

Name: Guru Dutt
Birth Date: 9 July 1925
Place: Padukone, India
Death Date: 10 October 1964
Place: Mumbai, India

By the mid-1950s, Guru Dutt, the maestro film-maker, had already established himself commercially with four big hits, romantic comedies and thrillers. He even had two hit films as a lead actor. However, *Pyaasa* was the story he had been pining to tell on the big screen for nearly a decade now but hadn't been successful earlier because of the story's artistic bent. He had written the original story based on his father's struggles as well as his early days in Mumbai. Of course, the story had undergone several changes to make it more relevant to the screens of the mid-1950s.

As hours ticked by in the AP Kardar studio on that mahurat day (an auspicious day on which the first shot of a movie is canned), Guru Dutt wondered why the film's hero, Dilip Kumar, hadn't turned up. The mahurat time for the film was ending. At 3 p.m., he decided to play the film's hero—a big risk. But the gamble paid off handsomely and his role in the movie is recognized as one of the greatest ever performances and *Pyaasa* is considered today as one of India's finest achievements. In fact, one cannot recall *Pyaasa* without also thinking of Guru Dutt! It is also equally difficult to accept all the classics that never came into existence because this maestro left the world at a young age.

Guru Dutt was born to Vasanthi and Shivashankar Padukone. He spent his early childhood in Bengal and was proficient in Konkani, English and Bengali. A sensitive child, Dutt was a dreamer and a bookworm. He was always inclined towards different forms of art, like *jatras* (gypsy theatre enacting folk tales), the music and songs of Baul singers, shadow plays (using fingers to create shadow figures) after the lamps were lit in the evenings. He also loved to dance and wanted to become a dancer once he grew up.

Guru Dutt worked as a telephone operator before landing a job at Prabhat Film Company, where he worked for three years. Post that, he started writing stories in English that were published in a local magazine. A couple of years later, he, along with his friend Dev Anand, whom he had met at Prabhat Company, made two blockbuster movies together in a row: *Baazi* and *Jaal*. This was just the beginning of an illustrious, though short, career.

Guru Dutt's creative abilities and his romance with the camera produced a string of cult classic movies, including *CID*, *Pyaasa*, *Aar Paar*, *Kaagaz ke Phool*, *Sahib Bibi Aur Ghulam*, and many more. *Kaagaz ke Phool* was the first Indian film produced in CinemaScope (a lens for shooting widescreen films and created by the president of 20th Century Fox). It required an elaborate process of securing the lens and a trip to Paris but Dutt was adamant. He was an all-rounder—a writer, actor, producer and director. Whichever hat he donned, he excelled. His desire to create artistic films and his cinematic expression made him produce the greatest hits of all time.

Guru Dutt married Geeta Ghosh Roy Chowdhury, who was a famous singer of her time. He had name, fame and wealth, yet he was melancholic. It is said that his real life often got reflected in his reel life. Maybe this was reflected in the song—

Ye mahalon, ye takhton, ye taajon ki duniya
Ye insaan ke dushman samaajon ki duniya
Ye daulat ke bhukhe rawaajon ki duniya
Ye duniya agar mil bhi jaaye to kya hai . . .

This melancholy probably led to his death at the young age of thirty-nine, leaving behind a weighty legacy.

The Messiah of Peace and Love

Name: Guru Nanak
Birth Date: 15 April 1469
Place: Talwandi village (present-day Pakistan)
Death Date: 22 September 1539
Place: Kartarpur (present-day Pakistan)

As per legend, it was late fifteenth century when Nanak's Janeu (thread ceremony) was performed in the Punjab state of present-day Pakistan. Seated on a platform facing the family pandit, amidst a healthy gathering of the guests, he couldn't quite focus. He had some questions.

When the pandit was about to initiate the ceremony, nine-year-old Nanak asked what a Janeu was and why he was being asked to wear one. Aware of his inquisitive nature, the pandit wasn't surprised. Nanak had a history of quizzing pandits and mullahs. The pandit explained the significance of the thread ceremony. He told him that it was almost like a second birth for those from the upper castes and it enabled a person to read Hindu religious texts. The Janeu was supposed to be spun by a Brahmin, with each cord representing different aspects of religious philosophy and worship.

However, there was no end to Nanak's difficult questions. Why was the thread not worn by females or those born in lower castes? Why did the ages at which the thread ceremony was performed differ based on the caste? Soon the pandit lost his cool and retorted that questioning religious practices was a sin. Nanak replied that using our God-given brain to question what we don't understand in religious scriptures cannot be a sin. He refused to wear the Janeu, saying it divided people on the basis of caste. Nanak said the sacred soul of Janeu could be achieved by 'making compassion the cotton, contentment the thread, modesty the knot and truth the twist'. If there was such a Janeu, he would be happy to put it on.

Young Nanak showed keen interest in religion and studied Islam and Hinduism. Later, he became a poet and a spiritual teacher and drew crowds of both Hindus and Muslims. Nanak's wisdom and teachings gave birth to the beliefs of Sikhism. His followers came to be known as Sikhs. Recognized as the founder of Sikhism and the first of the ten Sikh gurus, Guru Nanak's teachings attributed that there is only one God (*ik onkar*).

Nanak was born in a Hindu Khatri family in the year 1469 in a village, now known as Nankana Sahib in Pakistan. Exhibiting wisdom at the early age of five, Nanak was popularly called the 'divine' child. At fifteen, Nanak went to Sultanpur to stay with his sister Nanaki and her husband, who also helped him get a job. Later, he got married and had two sons.

During his formative years, Guru Nanak travelled far and wide, teaching that human beings can have direct access to God without rituals and that everyone, regardless of caste or gender, was equal in the eyes of God.

He died in 1539 in Kartarpur. It is believed that as Hindus and Muslims were fighting over his body, on removal of the cloth covering his dead body, they found only flowers!

Nanak's hymns were collected and recorded in the Adi Granth (Granth Sahib) by Guru Arjan, the fifth Sikh Guru, in 1604. It also contains hymns by other Sikh gurus. The book is written in Gurmukhi and is worshipped in gurdwaras all around the world.

It is said that, when he was young, Nanak decided to feed hungry men with the money his father had given him. He explained that by using the money to feed the needy, he had actually used it to get the highest return possible. His belief in selfless service (*seva*) led to the popularity of community kitchens, which was then named 'langar' in the Sikh tradition. Today, langars are offered by every gurdwara in the world and remain open to everyone, irrespective of faith, gender, caste, class or religion.

Guru Nanak encouraged social justice, unity of mankind and prosperity of all. His birth is celebrated worldwide as Guru Nanak Jayanti or Guru Nanak Gurupurab.

The Italian Odissi

Name: Ileana Citaristi
Place of birth: Italy

Ileana grew up in Italy and when she was a child, much to her chagrin, her classical ballet classes were cut short by her conservative family so that she could focus on studies. When she started going to college during the late 1960s, a wave of student-led rebellion was sweeping Italy, mirroring the protest movements across different European nations. In particular, students from the Italian working and peasant sections exposed to modern education and culture were protesting against the traditional society which harboured a capitalist and patriarchal mindset.

Ileana got hooked to the movement against rules, authorities and boundaries in Italy, having found an outlet to rebel against whatever was imposed on her by religion and society. As a result, her dance aspirations were on the backburner during that period.

Subsequently, while studying Eastern philosophy in college, she realized that the dance, which had paused for her many years ago, was still alive in her mind and body. The desire to express herself led her to physical theatre (where storytelling is done primarily through physical movement). Around that time, Ileana witnessed a Kathakali dance performance by an artist from Kerala who had travelled to Italy for the performance. Ileana was awestruck by the facial and bodily movements of the artist, each of which seemed to have a distinct meaning. She was enamoured by this form of expression. After speaking to the performing artist, Ileana took up a three-month workshop.

At the end of three months, she was elated at being exposed to Kathakali. She asked the artist who was now her guru what she could do next, and he suggested Odissi.

On her visit to India, which she had planned for a year, she thought about spending the first six months in Odisha, followed by another six months in Kerala learning Kathakali. So, she headed straight to Odisha for the first leg of her tour and enrolled under Kelucharan Mohapatra, the legendary Odissi dancer. Ileana had no idea that Odissi would absorb her so profoundly that everything else would turn irrelevant and that the six months would swell to six years before she would visit Italy. Under her guru, Kelucharan, Ileana would be reborn as an acclaimed Odissi dancer and become entwined with the cultural fabric of India.

Ileana settled in Odisha in 1979 and learnt about the people and the diverse cultures of India. Apart from learning Odissi, she also mastered Mayurbhanj Chhau (a dance form from east India) under the tutelage of Guru Hari Nayak and holds the title of 'Acharya' from the Sangeet Mahavidyalaya of Bhubaneswar. She also has a doctorate of philosophy and has conducted researches on psychoanalysis and Eastern mythology.

As a result of having a creative bent, Ileana did a lot of innovations in Odissi and Chhau. Her productions cover themes from all across the world: Greek mythology, Japanese haiku, Chinese yin and yang and even personalities like Mother Teresa. According to her, 'My choreographies are never prosaic. I use poetry and make it suggestive. I like to leave some space so that the person who receives it uses his/her imagination to fill that space. The works we are going to present are all aphorisms I found somewhere or the other. All are natural reflections of what we desire or aspire to be. How we choose the subject of our work and how we treat them speaks volumes about us as choreographers.'

She is also the founder of Art Vision Academy, established in Bhubaneswar in 1996. The academy promotes art and culture through dance and other art forms like theatre, painting and many more. Ileana has performed all over the world and is the recipient of several national and international awards. She became the first dancer of foreign origin to receive the Padma Shri in the year 2006.

Powerful Corporate Leader

Name: Indra Nooyi
Birth Date: 28 October 1955
Place: Chennai, India

Indra Nooyi had already been the CEO of PepsiCo for more than three years, when in November 2009 she found herself engaged in several meetings with two dozen top business executives from the US and India; a high-level Indian delegation was visiting the US. Soon Barack Obama (erstwhile President of the US) and Manmohan Singh (erstwhile prime minister of India) entered the room to understand what progress the group of business leaders had made. The US President proceeded with introducing the American members to the Indian PM. When Obama got to Indra, Manmohan Singh exclaimed, 'Oh! But she is one of us!' The US President flashed a big smile and said without missing a beat, 'Ah, but she is one of us, too!' This dichotomy perfectly defines one of the most powerful corporate leaders ever, who straddles two vastly different worlds and is widely admired in both. Indra's cultural roots and her connection to India always remained strong. At the same time, she is also the woman who started the second chapter of her life at twenty-three in the US and ascended to be an iconic leader of an iconic company. Another duality that has defined Indra is the twin demands of family and work that she has juggled throughout her corporate life.

Indra believes that no matter how big the professional achievements, none of us are just professionals. She believes if you want to get the best out of people, you have to let them bring their whole selves to work. 'I've always tried to accommodate the whole person,' she says. 'I talk to people about their family, about any issues they're going through, and I like to explore how the company can alleviate some of the issues. You need to show empathy as a leader.'

Indra Nooyi, who shone as one of the most iconic corporate leaders, devised mechanisms within PepsiCo to support employees so that they can take care of their families. The aim is to help employees not just to build a career but also a life.

Her mantra at the time when she headed PepsiCo was 'Be a lifelong student, don't lose your curiosity.'

Ranked among the world's 100 most powerful women, after her post-graduation from IIM, Kolkata, she shifted to the USA, where she earned a master's degree from the Yale School of Management. She joined PepsiCo in 1994, and within a dozen years, reached the much-coveted post of CEO. The carefree girl who loved playing cricket and guitar in an all-girl rock band back in India was now considered a game changer in a leading global company.

Indra was not just a professional but also a trendsetter. At PepsiCo, she diversified the product portfolio by classifying PepsiCo products into three categories: 'fun for you' (junk), 'better for you' (low-fat/diet snacks) and 'good for you' (healthy options). She reshaped the perception around junk food by introducing healthier choices. This was a tactical risk that paid off. She believes, 'The world is full of ideas today, and if we don't do it, someone else will. In order to do that, we have to allow people to be bold, and write rules in any way they want to.'

Apart from her strategies, Indra championed sustainable development too. Packaging at PepsiCo was redesigned to reduce and recycle waste and conserve water and non-renewable energy resources.

Indra retired from her post at PepsiCo in 2018. Today, she is a member of the board of directors of Amazon and is the first independent female director of the International Cricket Council (ICC).

Indra Nooyi truly defied the limitations that society often puts on young girls so they don't dream big, or dream at all.

Iron Lady of Manipur

Name: Irom Sharmila
Birth Date: 14 March 1972
Place: Imphal, India

On 2 November 2000, twenty-eight-year-old Irom Sharmila had gone out to attend a seminar titled 'Internal Cultural Peace', the venue being a few kilometres from her home in Imphal.

When she returned in the evening, Irom heard about the tragedy that had unfolded in Malom, near the Imphal airport. Innocent civilians had been gunned down by the Assam Rifles (a paramilitary force) on the pretext of an insurgent encounter. Manipur and other north-eastern states had the Armed Forces Special Powers Act (AFSPA) enforced, under which the Indian Army has special powers to arrest, use force or even open fire, enter or search certain premises without a warrant to ensure peace in the region. Sharmila had always been concerned about the problems that besieged Manipur and had participated in social action.

Just a couple of days before the Malom incident, she had completed her internship with Human Rights Alert—a highly respected human rights organization. But the incident in Malom made her feel that the protests were not helping the cause.

That night, she tossed and turned before reaching a decision on what she would do in her individual capacity.

Over the next two days, she told her family, including her mother and brother, about the decision, 'I will not eat until AFSPA is withdrawn from Manipur.' On 5 November 2000, she made her vow public during a meeting of Universal Youth Development Council (UYDC). She would be arrested within a week for the crime of attempting suicide. And these cycles of arresting and force-feeding would continue for a whopping sixteen years before she would break her fast in August 2016, when she would end her vow, disillusioned with AFSPA still continuing.

Irom was born in 1972, the same year Manipur got full statehood. Fondness for reading during her childhood made her aware of the troubles her homeland was in. While reading textbooks, several questions churned in her mind: why there was no mention of north-eastern states in India's struggle for freedom, why India's infrastructural development since 1947 did not reflect in her state, why there was so much poverty and illiteracy and almost zero social development in her region, why insurgency was spreading like wildfire, and so on. This is probably why she took up journalism after completing school. She wrote articles and a column for *Hueiyen Lanpao*, a local daily. It was during these days that she started writing poetry. In the twelfth year of her fasting, she wrote a thousand-word poem titled *Birth*, which is narrative in nature and covers her experiences and vision.

Always interested in social service, she joined various social groups and worked for the betterment of the region and its people. While pursuing her internship at Human Rights Alert, she met the victims of the unfortunate clashes with the army. She also met other social workers, media persons and scholars who attended to these victims. These meetings affected her so much that she decided to take the big step.

Sixteen years later, after the breaking of her fast, Irom launched a political party. However, she didn't succeed in politics and therefore left it after a couple of years to settle down and raise a family. Though Irom didn't achieve her objective, she gained international recognition and respect as an icon of public protest against state atrocities. Irom dared to do what she wanted to do for the people of her state. Her relentless fight against the system has inspired many to pick up the baton that she left behind.

Grand Doyenne of Urdu Literature

Name: Ismat Chughtai
Birth Date: 21 August 1915
Place: Budaun, India
Death Date: 24 October 1991
Place: Mumbai, India

By the 1940s, Ismat Chughtai had already earned a name as a writer who took on bold themes that irked the puritanical. But when her doorbell rang one evening, she was least expecting a police officer to arrive with a summons from the Lahore High Court. Ismat had been charged with obscenity for her short story 'Lihaaf' (The Quilt) and she was required to appear before the court on the appointed day, failing which strict action would be taken against her.

A few 'concerned' citizens had directed the government's attention to her story, saying it was morally damaging for it portrayed an intimate relationship between two women. The first court hearing in January 1945 led to the second one in November 1946. On the day of the hearing, the court was crowded. People had advised Ismat to apologize in court for her story and had offered to pay any court-imposed fine on her behalf if she apologized.

However, she was known to stand by her stories. Eventually, things turned Ismat's way when the witnesses testifying against the book could not withstand her lawyer's cross-examination. The detractor lobby wanted to pick a condemnable word from the book, but no such word could stand the test of the defendant lawyer's questions. Finally, the judge said that he had read many of her stories and had found nothing obscene in them or in 'Lihaaf'. Ismat won the case.

Today, widely recognized as one of the four pillars of modern Urdu literature, Ismat Chughtai's name still echoes as a realist author of the twentieth century. She penned some of the most challenging and fascinating female characters.

Being born and brought up in a large middle-class Muslim family in Uttar Pradesh revealed to Ismat the oppressive nature of the society at an early age. To rebel became her second nature. She fought to study further than the eighth standard when her parents wanted her to stop studying and learn the ropes of homemaking. She continued studying and defied every stereotype imposed on her by doing what her brothers did, like climbing trees, playing street football and horseback riding. She did everything that girls were forbidden to do.

While studying at Aligarh Muslim University, Ismat joined the Progressive Writers' Association and wrote short stories in Urdu that portrayed the complexities of a woman's mind. After finishing her studies, she worked as the headmistress of a school and subsequently an inspector of schools in Mumbai. All the while, she never stopped writing stories.

Ismat was a fierce feminist writer who didn't think much of controversies arising out of her writings—they exposed the double standards and the hypocrisies of society. Ismat picked up characters and plots from real life around her, 'I write about people I know or have known. What should a writer write about anyway?' While on one hand, her stories revolved around Hindu and Muslim traditions (purdah, child widows, sati, etc.), religious intolerances, female identity crisis, male supremacy and female subjugation, on the other hand, they also celebrated life—the cultural richness, large families, the confusions, the tears and the laughter, squabbles within families and with neighbours.

Ismat authored many short stories, plays, film scripts and novels. Her novels include *Masooma* (The Innocent Girl), *Saudai* (Obsession), *Dil ki Duniya* (The Heart Breaks Free), *Tedhi Lakeer* (The Crooked Line), *Ajeeb Aadmi* (A Very Strange Man) and *Jangli Kabootar* (Wild Pigeons). They explored the themes of social divide and injustices, economic disparity, sexual exploitation, tangled emotional lives of people in the film industry, lives of women in a community. Ismat, along with her husband, wrote, directed and produced films like *Ziddi*, *Arzoo*, *Sone ki Chidiya* and *Fareb* together. *Garm Hava*, the famous film made about the Indo-Pak Partition, was also written by Chughtai.

Ismat remained a true rebel against the norms even after her death. Since she was 'scared of being buried', she was cremated as per her wish. Awarded the Padma Shri in 1976, Chughtai's stories and exceptional candour continues to charm her readers. Her works also continue to find new readers in every new generation.

Master of Science

Name: Jagadish Chandra Bose
Birth Date: 30 November 1858
Place: Bikrampur, India
Death Date: 23 November 1937
Place: Giridh, India

Late nineteenth century

J.C. Bose impressed the viceroy of India, Lord Ripon, when he returned to India after securing three degrees from the prestigious University of Cambridge. However, British administrators, due to their racial policy, were reluctant to offer Bose a post at Imperial Educational Service (IES). They believed Indians were incapable of understanding exact sciences, let alone train students.

Bose put his foot down and refused to accept Provincial Service, which they willingly offered instead. Therefore, upon Ripon's intervention, Bose was appointed to educational service as the officiating professor of physics at Presidency College, Calcutta. He was, however, offered only half the salary of what English professors would receive for the same position. A defiant Bose took up the job but decided not to take the monthly salary as a protest against the discriminatory policy of the British.

During that period, Bose faced significant personal challenges as his family was ridden with the old debts of his father, so much so that family properties were sold to repay debts. But Bose stood firm and eventually won the fight.

Sir Alfred Croft, the director of Public Instruction, and the principal, C.H. Tawney, were impressed by Bose's commitment to teaching and how well he could maintain students' discipline. But most importantly, they appreciated how well he stood up for what he believed was right. Bose's salary was brought on par with the English professors and his position was made permanent.

This indomitable spirit of Bose stood him in good stead throughout his career as he had to take on scientists who looked down upon Asian scientists.

J.C. Bose was brought up in an affluent family. His father loved science. He was a philanthropist and a follower of Brahmo Samaj (casteless religion). It was these principles that led him to admit Jagadish to a non-English school where underprivileged children studied. Bose's father believed it was important to know one's mother tongue and people before mastering English. Only when Jagadish turned eleven was he sent to the best school in the country, mainly set up for English boys. Speaking about his vernacular school later, Jagadish once said, 'At that time, sending children to English schools was an aristocratic status symbol. In the vernacular school, to which I was sent, the son of the Muslim attendant of my father sat on my right side, and the son of a fisherman sat on my left. They were my playmates.' He also credited the school as the place where he developed a keen interest in the 'workings of nature'.

After finishing his schooling at St. Xavier's, Jagadish left for the University of Cambridge, where he studied physics, chemistry and botany from eminent personalities like Lord Rayleigh, recipient of the Nobel Prize for discovering argon, and Sir Francis Darwin, a botanist and the son of Charles Darwin. He came back to India and taught students for many years.

Later, he made significant discoveries in wireless signalling (many acknowledge that this was the seed that grew into modern Wi-Fi technology) and the detection of radio signals.

Bose was among the pioneers of research in radio technology. It is believed that he demonstrated, for the first time ever, wireless communication using radio waves, although Italian physicist Guglielmo Marconi is credited with developing the first proper system of radio communication in 1897.

In fact, he also used Bose's scientific contribution to send the first wireless message across the Atlantic Ocean in 1901. The debate remains open to new revelations.

Perhaps Marconi is credited with the development of radio technology because Bose was against patenting. He believed knowledge should be available to everyone and not constrained by patenting. As a result, despite his extensive research, his name is almost 'forgotten'. When asked by his nephew who the real inventor of the radio was, Bose said, 'It is not the inventor but the invention that matters.'

Bose also made progress in botany too. He invented the crescograph, a device that is used for measuring growth in plants and the environmental effects on them.

Much later, he established the Bose Institute in Kolkata and served as its director until his death in 1937. Bose donned many hats and achieved excellence as a biologist, botanist, polymath, biophysicist. To acknowledge his achievements in the field of wireless telecommunications, a crater on the moon has been named after Bose.

The Founder of Delhi Public School

Name: James Douglas Tytler
Birth Date: 31 March 1898
Place: Scotland, United Kingdom
Death Date: 13 September 1973
Place: New Delhi, India

When James Douglas Tytler arrived in India as chaplain to the viceroy attached to the Cathedral Church of Redemption, New Delhi, he was aghast to see the plight of poor children. His compassion urged him to help them and thus started his first school in 1941, within the compounds of the church. Classes were held in tents and under the trees. Sports like tennis, hockey, football, cricket, badminton, basketball and volleyball were played on the church fields.

James aimed to serve the helpless and to bridge the gap between the haves and have-nots. He believed that all kids should be loved, nurtured and accepted unconditionally.

As the school overcame challenge after challenge and continued to grow under his leadership, it caught the attention of eminent teachers from other schools.

Within five years, by 1946, many excellent teachers and students joined James's school. Post-Independence in 1947, after facing resistance from the church to let the school continue in the church compound, J.D. took the school out of the church premises and renamed it Naveen Bharat School (meaning 'New India School').

India was changing at that time and this change was reflected in the school system too. J.D. decided to give his school an overhaul and thus became instrumental in setting up the Delhi Public School Society. The first school became operational on Mathura Road, Delhi, in 1949. J.D. continued as its principal for three years before leaving it to establish several other schools.

Today, the DPS Society has schools spread over several countries. D. Kapilash, a teacher during that period, remembers, 'Children really loved him and he in turn got their undivided love. The little ones ran after him. He picked them up and gave them a piggy ride. You could see the kids holding his hands, clinging on his legs or sitting on his shoulders . . . He not only loved the children but also cared for and respected the teachers.' James was affectionately called 'Lal Murgi' (red hen) by kids as his face would turn red whenever he was happy or stern, as the situation warranted.

James was full of life and had a multifaceted persona. He was an educationist, a sports enthusiast and a patron of arts and music. He was a popular personality in Delhi society and people often sought his suggestions. His eagerness to help earned him the sobriquet of 'Good Samaritan of Delhi Sport'. He later worked as the president of the Delhi Olympic Association, Delhi Swimming Association, Delhi Weightlifting Association, the vice president of Delhi Gymnastics Association and a patron of the Delhi Cycling Association.

Not limiting himself to the educational and sports societies, James associated himself with the drama societies too. A lover of theatre, he sometimes acted on the stage and even in a film titled *Shakespeare Wallah*. He was the founder–member of several theatre groups and also the Delhi Music Society.

James Tytler was a visionary who fell in love with India and sought its citizenship; in exchange he gave to India a robust modern school system.

Charming Actress, Trailblazing Politician

Name: Jayalalithaa Jayaram
Birth Date: 24 February 1948
Place: Melukote, Karnataka, India
Death Date: 5 December 2016
Place: Chennai, India

The day 25 March 1989 started like any other for Jayalalithaa as she entered the Tamil Nadu Assembly as the leader of the opposition. Little did she know that the day would stand out in the history of Indian politics.

It started with the chief minister, M. Karunanidhi, trying to present the state budget and Jayalalithaa seeking a breach of privilege (there are certain rights and immunities enjoyed by the members of Parliament and when any of these rights are disregarded, the offence is called a breach of privilege) motion against him for the phone tapping and police high-handedness she had been subjected to in the preceding days. One thing led to another, and the arguments soon turned into an ugly brawl with those in power and the opposition trading blows.

It was complete mayhem inside the Tamil Nadu Assembly.

Jayalalithaa, too, came under attack. Those against her pulled her hair and hurled mics, bundles of paper and whatever else they could lay their hands on. To make matters worse, as she was being escorted out of the assembly by her party workers, someone pulled at her saree. An infuriated Jayalalithaa left the assembly in tears, but she also took a vow that changed the course of her political life and Tamil Nadu politics.

She swore that she would enter the Tamil Nadu Assembly again only as the state's chief minister.

True to her word, two years later, in 1991, she entered the assembly as the chief minister of the state. Such was the determination of one of the strongest leaders that the state had seen.

At the age of two, Jayalalithaa had lost her father. Her mother left her with her grandparents and aunt in Mysuru, and relocated to Chennai to earn a living in the film industry. She joined her mother only after her aunt got married.

Jayalalithaa was always an intelligent child, she excelled at school and even won the state-level gold medal in her tenth-board exams. An all-rounder, she was trained in Carnatic and Western classical music. She could play the piano flawlessly and learnt Bharatanatyam,

Kuchipudi, Mohiniattam, Manipuri dance and Kathak forms. However, she discontinued her studies to pursue her interest in the film industry.

While still at school, she had started acting in plays and movies. Influenced by her mother, and due to financial difficulties, she jumped into the industry full-time, though she strongly desired to be a lawyer. Jayalalithaa was good at whatever she did, and had a string of blockbuster movies in southern cinema, many of which were female-centric. After nearly two decades in the film industry, she voluntarily bid farewell to the cine world to pursue 'other things'.

Jayalalithaa joined politics in the early 1980s. She was always a poised and polished politician who articulated her thoughts and opinions very well. She played her role in the opposition impeccably. Taking charge as the chief minister in 1991 for the first time, she held the position for six terms till her death in 2016.

Jayalalithaa's legacy as a politician lingers on. She introduced several citizen welfare initiatives during her tenure as the chief minister, including subsidized 'Amma' food items, medicines, cement, canteens and many more. Tamil Nadu saw rapid development in terms of infrastructure and industry during her ruling years, resulting in increased employment and better quality of life.

No wonder she is still remembered as 'Amma', a mother figure, by the people of Tamil Nadu.

The Second Rani of Jhansi

Name: Jhalkari Bai
Birth Date: 22 November 1830
Place: Jhansi, India
Death Date: 4 April 1858
Place: Jhansi, India

It is said that in 1858 the British Army, commanded by Hugh Rose, had surrounded the Jhansi Fort, bombarding it from all sides. There was little doubt about the invading army overrunning the fort and hence, saving Rani Lakshmi Bai and her little son Damodar was the need of the hour. The rani mounted her horse with her son in tow, reached the palace walls and leapt out into the dark night to safety. But at the same time, the rani with a turban and a crescent mark on her forehead was also inside the fort, fighting the British valiantly.

How could the same person be in two places?

Well, the rani resisting the invaders inside the fort was Jhalkari Bai—the queen's able adviser and lookalike. In physique, complexion and even eye colour, she was so much like the queen that it was impossible to tell them apart when dressed similarly. Jhalkari successfully distracted the invaders, allowing Rani Lakshmi Bai to escape and regroup with other warriors. The fort did fall eventually and the British imprisoned Jhalkari, thinking she was the queen. It took them some time to figure out who she actually was, perhaps betrayed by a traitor in the fort who revealed her true identity. What happened to this brave alter ego of the Rani subsequently is not known for certain. One version says she died at the hands of the British in 1858 during the uprising. As per a second version, the British set her free and she lived to be old.

Despite being a second Rani of Jhansi while fighting the British, she's an oft-forgotten figure or simply a footnote in Rani Lakshmi Bai's story. The rani was aided in key battles by the legendary Dalit woman warrior, Jhalkari Bai, who rose from a humble background to an accomplished warrior and the queen's trusted adviser.

Jhalkari Bai was born to Sadoba Singh and Jamuna Devi in Bhojla village near Jhansi in 1830. Her parents belonged to the Kori community and were weavers. Since the family income was meagre, she didn't get a chance to study in a formal school. After her mother passed away, her father took good care of his only child and raised Jhalkari into a fearless woman. She learnt the art of weaponry and horse riding at an early age. Legend says that she even fought a tiger once and a leopard with a stick. Her adventurous and brave spirit made her a household name in Jhansi.

Young Jhalkari, after meeting Rani Lakshmi Bai, joined her battalion of women warriors called Durga Dal. She proved herself to be a master strategist and fought dauntlessly in the freedom struggle that took place in 1858. The tales of Jhalkari Bai's courage have been passed across generations. Though there is little literature to tell us more about this valiant woman, she is popularly known to all as Veerangana, who had died defending her queen and the country.

The people of Bundelkhand fondly remember her through poems like:

Macha Jhansi mein ghamasan, chahun aur machee kilkari thee,
Angrezon se loha lenein, ran mein kudee Jhalkari thee.

(Amidst the sound and fury of the battle at Jhansi, Jhalkari plunged herself into the battlefield to confront the British.)

The Rocket Man of India

Name: Kailasavadivoo Sivan
Birth Date: 14 April 1957
Place: Kanyakumari district, India

Back in the early seventies, Sivan, a farmer's son from Tamil Nadu, had completed two years of a pre-university course and dreamed of enrolling in an engineering course for his graduation. The boy had studied at Tamil-medium schools in his village and had subsequently studied at a college in Nagercoil for two years.

Throughout his academic life, Sivan's father had ensured that the boy helped out on the fields as well as in mango orchards (during harvest season) before and after school or college. In fact, his father's criterion for selecting the educational institutions was proximity to their place so that his bright son could always lend an additional hand at work. So after his pre-university course, when

Sivan said he wanted to study engineering, the request was denied because the course was too costly to afford. Sivan was determined to pursue it and, as a mark of protest, went on a hunger strike for a week. However, his father still didn't budge. Finally, Sivan had to give in and decided to pursue a bachelor's degree in science at the same college, studying maths, physics and statistics while also helping his father in the fields.

Always fascinated by aircrafts, Sivan once said in an interview that he and his friends would make aircrafts out of mud taken from the fields. This fascination made him want to study them. At the end of his BSc, he applied to Madras Institute of Technology (MIT) following his uncle's advice. This time around, Sivan's father supported his son and even sold a part of his fields to pay his college fees. Though he stammered during the interview, Sivan was accepted to the course of aeronautical engineering at MIT as he had received full marks in his core subjects in BSc.

After that, there was no looking back for Sivan, who had had humble beginnings. Post engineering, he completed his post-graduation from the Indian Institute of Science, Bengaluru. Eventually, he ended up at Indian Space Research Organisation (ISRO), where he developed a reputation as a renowned scientist and also completed his PhD along the way. He played a critical role in several milestones in ISRO's history. From developing cryogenic engines to launch vehicles and charting cost-effective strategies for the

Mars Orbiter Mission (MOM) in 2014, to simulating a 6D trajectory software named SITARA, setting a world record for ISRO by launching 104 satellites together in 2017 and getting a snag fixed in Chandrayaan-2 within twenty-four hours, his contributions have earned him the sobriquet 'the Rocket Man of India'. The crowning glory of his career was when he was appointed the head of ISRO.

Dr Sivan is an epitome of simple living and innovative thinking—he has proposed using space technologies for developing advanced medical devices. The aim is to create automated artificial limbs and organs. He initiated talks with industry partners and the wheels have been set in motion.

Sivan projects a conviction borne by experience and practice. One of the big lessons that life taught him, he says, is, 'Whenever something is denied to you, something bigger is waiting for you.' He did not let coming from a humble background, a vernacular medium and the absence of foreign education get in the way of achieving resounding success in life. His life is an exemplary example of how we must simply try our best instead of fretting over missed opportunities.

The Guardian Angel

Name: Kailash Satyarthi
Birth Date: 11 January 1954
Place: Vidisha, India

At five, Kailash was excited to attend his first day at school. Near the school gate, he noticed a cobbler polishing shoes along with his small boy, who stared expectantly at passers-by hoping for more work. Once he reached his class, Kailash asked his teacher why the cobbler's boy wasn't in school with them. The teacher said the boy belonged to a poor family and, for them, working from a young age was a necessity. Not convinced, he posed the same question to the school's headmaster but got the same reply.

A week or so passed by, and with time, Kailash had gathered enough courage to approach the cobbler directly. After school one day, he asked the cobbler, 'Why don't you send your son to school?' The cobbler replied that right from the days of his great-grandfather, their family had been mending shoes. He added pitifully, 'You don't know, Babuji, we people are born to only work.'

Though little Kailash didn't completely understand what the cobbler had said, he did wonder why some kids were born to work, whereas others like him had the option of dreaming and even chasing those dreams. The interaction with the cobbler changed the way he saw the world. It made him realize there was disparity all around. As he grew up, he became a guardian angel who launched several crusades to make the world a better place for underprivileged children.

Kailash spent his childhood in Vidisha in Madhya Pradesh. Although born with the privileges that children around him had, he was a little different from the others. While other children were engrossed in books and playthings, Kailash observed the world he inhabited. As he grew up, he started questioning the social fabric of society. He became aware of the hypocrisy that the political, social and religious leaders exhibited. After acquiring a degree in electrical engineering, he could have secured a job anywhere. Instead, he decided to teach, with the hope of changing society. But he couldn't make a dent.

So in 1980, he launched the Bachpan Bachao Andolan (Save Childhood Movement)—the first of its kind in India. The aim was to save children from child labour and slavery by enabling them to claim the right to education. In the last four decades, Kailash's movements and organizations have saved almost a hundred thousand children from child labour, human trafficking, slavery and exploitation.

Not restricted to India, his efforts have reaped fruits around the world, from the formation of the South Asian Coalition on Child Servitude in 1989 to RugMark (now GoodWeave), aimed at reducing the use of child labour in the rug-making industry. With a series of demonstrations and marches, children have been rescued from industries like firecracker making, the circus, rug weaving, bangle making, brassware and lock making, embroidery, stone quarries and many others. Rescuing children from such places was not easy. Kailash and his team were often beaten, abused, their houses ransacked, and a couple of them even lost their lives. However, this never stopped Kailash and his team.

One of his notable achievements has been establishing Bal Mitra Grams (BMGs) in India and Nepal. Here, children are actively involved in decision-making in villages, for example, a parliamentary session led by children works with the village panchayat to address child-related issues. Kailash has also established several educational and rehabilitation centres, which have changed many lives. Kailash has received several awards, among them is the Nobel Peace Prize, which he shared with Malala Yousafzai 'for their struggle against the suppression of children and young people and for the right of all children to education.'

According to Kailash, 'If a child is denied education and forced to work instead, violence has been inflicted. If a child and its parents are denied opportunities for a promising tomorrow, violence has been inflicted. If a child reels under poverty, violence has been inflicted. If obstacles are laid in the path of a child, inhibiting her progress and development, violence has been inflicted.'

The Versatile Actor

Name: Kamal Haasan
Birth Date: 7 November 1954
Place: Paramakudi, India

In the late 1950s, barely four, little Kamal travelled with his mother to Chennai from his native village, Paramakudi. Kamal's mother had undertaken this trip as part of her treatment and the boy was sent along with an intent to have him enrolled in a convent school. While in Chennai, a doctor friend of the family took Kamal to a film party. Encouraged by elders, the little boy narrated a dialogue from a movie of the legendary Sivaji Ganesan.

Incidentally, a well-known producer was looking for a child artist for a new film at the same party. Impressed by Kamal, the producer signed him for the role in *Kalathur Kannamma*. Little Kamal's portrayal of an innocent child against the backdrop of societal discrimination stole the audience's hearts and he went on to win the President's Gold Medal for his role. Critics noted Haasan's natural expressions and composure in front of the camera at such a young age.

The boy seemed set to carve his own niche in the world of cinema, which he did in style by becoming one of the most versatile actors of his age and playing iconic roles cutting across languages—dwarf, woman, drunkard, patriot and Bharatanatyam dancer, to name a few. However, it wasn't a smooth progression into the world of cinema beyond his first movie.

As he grew up, Kamal developed a keen interest in dance as a diversion from studies and was giving stage performances when he broke his leg. He was out of action for quite some time. During that period, someone approached him to be a dance choreographer in a film, a job that connected him back to the film world. One thing led to another, and before turning twenty, he had performed his first adult role in the movie *Arangetram*, which was released in 1973.

The next twenty years saw him acting in numerous films, many of which were blockbusters. In addition to Tamil, he has also acted in Hindi, Telugu, Kannada, Malayalam and Bengali films. He not only acted in but also wrote, produced and directed films. Some of the noted films he wrote are: *Raja Paarvai*, *Hey Ram*, *Nala Damayanthi*, *Dasavathaaram*, *Manmadan Ambu* and *Vishwaroopam*. As a playback singer he has composed many songs too. An interest in technical aspects of film-making led him to learn the art of makeup in the

United States and even train for the same under Michael Westmore (known for his work on the iconic *Star Trek*).

Kamal is deeply involved with social work. He consistently urges his fans to contribute to social services and has formed the Kamal Narpani Iyakkam (Kamal Welfare Association), in which his fan clubs organize donation drives. He is the first recipient of the Abraham Kovoor National Award in 2004 for being a secular artist. He has also been conferred with many national and international awards, including the National Film Award (four times), the Padma Shri (1990) and the Padma Bhushan (2014).

An eternal learner, he believes, 'I'd like to keep updating myself. That's the only way to make life interesting. And because I am a performer, I like to do it deliberately and with purpose.'

The Backyard Entrepreneur

Name: Karsanbhai Patel
Birth Date: 1945
Place: Mehsana, India

Gujarat, 1969

Karsanbhai Patel was a qualified science graduate who was working as a junior chemist in the geology and mining department of the state government. But he had bigger dreams for himself. Using his knowledge of chemistry, he was moonlighting in his backyard in the scorching heat of Ahmedabad, mixing soda ash and other intermediaries to create a new detergent powder.

The existing detergents in the domestic market were priced too high for the middle- and lower-income groups. Therein, he saw an opportunity to introduce a low-cost, 'value for money' product. Using bare hands, a bucket and, most importantly, a strong vision, he finally created a yellow powder that he packed in polythene bags and sold door-to-door on his way to the office on his bicycle. This revolutionary new detergent was priced at about Rs 3 per kg, thanks to indigenous processes, low-profile marketing and non-flashy packaging. The phosphate-free detergent, which Karsanbhai named Nirma after his daughter, was at least Rs 10 less than the cheapest detergent available in the market at that time.

Gradually, with a 'money back guarantee', the product became a hit in Ahmedabad. Buoyed by the initial success, Karsanbhai ventured full-time into entrepreneurship and spearheaded one of corporate India's most discussed success stories. Nirma, the detergent with clever marketing and brand positioning, became a hallmark of affordability and good value.

Karsanbhai was born into a family of farmers. Before venturing into full-time entrepreneurship, he worked as a lab technician. However, after successfully selling his indigenous detergent powder for three years, he felt confident enough to quit his regular job. Soon, Nirma became a popular name in Gujarat and Maharashtra. With his astute business acumen, Karsanbhai took bold decisions that revolutionized the detergent market and propelled his company to greater heights, supplying all over India and even in neighbouring countries.

The catchy Nirma jingle soon became a household earworm. There is an interesting story behind the iconic advertisement. In those days, it was normal to supply products on credit. Karsanbhai didn't want his money to get blocked. Therefore, in order to discourage creditors, he invested in this jingle, which played on the radio and television continuously for months. As a result, while there was a surge in demand in the market, Karsanbhai had stopped the supply. People flocked the markets, but the product was nowhere to be found. Consequently, shopkeepers pleaded with him to deliver the detergent. He obliged and made huge profits while on zero credit. Since then, he is known for his ingenuity in marketing and risk-taking abilities.

Today, Nirma is a major consumer brand that offers a wide range of detergents, soaps and personal care products, and edibles, with twenty-six different major manufacturing plants pan-India.

Self-made Karsanbhai recognizes the importance of education. As a result, in 1995, he established the Nirma Institute of Technology in Ahmedabad, and in 2003, the Institute of Management and the Nirma University of Science and Technology. He further contributed to the start-up ecosystem of India by establishing NirmaLabs in 2004, which trains and incubates budding entrepreneurs.

Karsanbhai believes that 'it is very important to enjoy one's work while doing it . . . to strive for excellence . . . to take the right decisions at the right time . . . to practise certain business ethics on the outside and at the same time, continue to grow', and this is what makes him an extraordinary businessman.

The Unsung Heroine

Name: Kasturba Gandhi
Birth Date: 11 April 1869
Place: Porbandar, India
Death Date: 22 February 1944
Place: Pune, India

Kasturba was married in her early teens in the 1880s and lived in Porbandar with her husband. In the early days of her marriage, Kasturba learnt that her husband had a passion for truth and lifelong faithfulness to her. She knew that Mohan expected her also to show the same faithfulness and this expectation made him jealous. He would always watch her movements, though there was no real reason to doubt her.

Kasturba didn't quite appreciate Mohan telling her that she shouldn't step out of the house without his permission. She was accommodative and a devoted wife, but she also had a proud and free spirit contrary to the society of the time. Kasturba chose not to oppose her husband's restrictions verbally. However, her mind remained unshackled and trips to the temple with her friends continued like earlier without Mohan's permission. Bitterness crept into their relationship and there were phases when the teen couple did not speak to each other.

Kasturba stood her ground and continued her peaceful opposition and finally made her husband realize that she was independent in her own way and would follow his decisions only out of conviction but not coercion, a quality that she retained till the end of her life. At the same time, Kasturba went out of her way to adjust to Mohan's strict way of life, helping him rise spiritually. Mohan would garner respect and emerge as Mahatma Gandhi—the towering leader of India's freedom struggle with worldwide following and recognition. But his pillar of strength, Kasturba, who made umpteen sacrifices and provided unstinted support to the Mahatma in his journey, has largely remained an unsung heroine.

Born into a prosperous merchant family in Porbandar, Kasturba Gandhi grew into a confident woman whose gentle demeanour was a cloak to a robust character. She was married to Mohandas Karamchand Gandhi in her teens and was known to put forward her thoughts since the beginning of their married life. While she supported him as was expected from women in those times, she never shied away from showing her displeasure at things she disagreed with.

Her companionship with Gandhi was not just in a relationship but also in his struggle for freedom. Accompanying him on his visits to various places, Kasturba Gandhi worked very hard to motivate women to fight for their rights and education, though she couldn't read or write well. She also taught them about the importance of health and hygiene. Fighting for the country's freedom, she took part in numerous protests and marches, for which she went to jail many times.

Affectionately called Ba by all, she served in ashrams too. She promoted khadi across villages and towns, sometimes walking for miles or travelling in bullock carts. Kasturba also played an active role in the Borsad Satyagraha of 1923–24 and the Bardoli Satyagraha of 1928. Bardoli paved a new way as it was the first time that the rural women participated in the freedom struggle. When Gandhiji started the boycott of the foreign goods, she actively participated in it. It is said that she burnt her favourite sari to show her support to the cause.

During one of the Quit India movement marches, in her powerful speech, Kasturba said—as Aparna Basu wrote in her biography of Kasturba Gandhi (titled *Kasturba Gandhi*)—'The women of India have to prove their mettle. They should all join in this struggle, regardless of caste or creed. Truth and non-violence must be our watchwords.' When she was imprisoned in Aga

Khan Palace in Pune for participating in the Quit India movement, her health deteriorated severely and India lost her only three years before gaining independence. But her efforts during the freedom struggle are still remembered today.

Master Entertainer

Name: Kishore Kumar
Birth Date: 4 August 1929
Place: Khandwa, India
Death Date: 13 October 1987
Place: Mumbai, India

Once, a director explained to the actor Kishore that he needed to drive along a certain path and exit the frame as part of the scene. Kishore followed the director's instructions verbatim, to the extent that he did not stop at all. The director wondered where Kishore had disappeared. He got a call from the actor some time later, asking if the shot was okay. Apparently, Kishore had continued driving and had reached Panvel, a town outside Mumbai, since the director never yelled 'Cut' to end the scene!

Such mischiefs are abundant in number, typifying the prankster we know as Kishore Kumar. Even as a singer, Kishore used to 'perform' the song, often jumping around like the actual actor would do on the screen to better capture the spirit of the song. For the iconic song, 'Dakiya Daak Laya' from the movie *Palkon ki Chhaon Mein*, the music director had to arrange for a bicycle while recording the song so that he could ring the bell on the handlebar and prance about while singing, like an actual postman!

A supreme performer who endeared himself to the masses by refusing to grow up, there will never be another quite like him.

From playing the tabla on his lawyer father's bald head to being a mischievous student at school, staging plays on a makeshift platform for other kids, Kishore was a born entertainer. Born as Abhas Kumar Ganguly, he was a free spirit. It is hard to believe now, but until the age of ten, Kishore Kumar's singing was called screechy by everyone—that was before his voice broke. However, he sang all the time, irrespective of how others reacted to his singing.

Well-liked at his college in Indore, he was popular due to his friendly nature and sense of humour. Boys would gather in his room every evening, singing songs from the latest movies, while Kishore played the harmonium. But this 'ruckus' cost him his college education, of which he was happy to let go.

His singing took him to Mumbai to join his elder brother Ashok Kumar, a well-known actor by then. Though Kishore acted in many films initially, he was never deeply interested in acting. Singing was his true passion.

Inspired by his role models like Rabindranath Tagore and singers K.L. Saigal, Jimmie Rodgers and Danny Kaye, Kishore mastered the art of yodelling (a form of singing that involves repeated and rapid changes of pitch) and created a string of superhit songs. He became a more popular singer than an actor, despite acting in many popular films.

Soon Kishore Kumar's songs would echo in every household. Most people would have a different emotion associated with his songs—to some his carefree singing brought joy, to others an inspiration to sing their hearts out. With a career spanning four decades, Kishore Kumar gave his audience a song for every mood, whether it was the life lessons ('Aanewala Pal Jaanewala Hai'), expressions of love ('O Hansini'), odes to friendships ('Tere Jaisa Yaar Kahaan') or war cries ('Aa Dekhen Zara'). Even today, his music continues to enchant new listeners and remains relevant.

Kishore Kumar died of a heart attack at the age of fifty-eight, leaving behind a long string of evergreen songs along with the unparalleled power and presence of his wondrous voice.

The Emperor from the Deccan

Name: Krishnadevaraya

A popular legend about Krishnadevaraya goes as follows:

It was the coronation ceremony in the kingdom of Vijayanagara in the early 1500s. A new king would soon ascend the lion throne. Timmarasu, the prime minister who was affectionately known as Appaji, was happy that Krishnadevaraya was taking over the reins of the kingdom. Appaji had been a father figure, coach and mentor to Krishnadevaraya. Legend says that before the coronation, Appaji asked to see the would-be king in private as there was one last teaching to be imparted. Once alone with his mentee, Appaji slapped him across the face, leaving Krishnadevaraya stunned for a moment, but he realized that there would be a lesson in this too. Appaji explained that the young king should never forget life's adversities and how painful punishments could be. Appaji concluded his final lesson by saying that after the coronation, he wouldn't have the right to discipline and would only be taking orders from the king. Krishnadevaraya graciously accepted the teaching.

Once the coronation rituals ended, the king summoned Appaji and other courtiers. The new king requested the group to instruct him about the court protocols and royal conduct. Appaji, along with the courtiers, gave him advice on conducting himself, running the state, dealing with enemies, avoiding vices. Krishnadevaraya understood that as a king, his aim should be to reward the good and punish the bad. He would need to be sensible while dispensing justice—how well he followed dharma would measure his success. He put these tenets of good governance into practice during his reign of two decades.

Legends and folk tales aside, Krishnadevaraya emerged as one of the greatest kings that ever ruled in the Indian subcontinent. It's only befitting that the devotees visiting Tirumala, one of the most visited religious places in the world, are greeted by a bronze statue of Krishnadevaraya at the temple entrance.

Krishnadevaraya was a magnificent king who ruled over the Vijayanagara empire in south India for twenty years (1509–1529). During his rule, Vijayanagara developed into a melting pot of cultures, where people from diverse backgrounds intermingled and saw growth together. This gave rise to a robust environment where almost everyone thrived. It is believed that trade was at its best in south India during Krishnadevaraya's reign. He was an excellent general who led his army to defeat sultans of Bijapur, Golconda and Bahamani and Gajapatis of Odisha. He united various regions within the boundaries of Vijayanagara. The administration under Krishnadevaraya was excellent as he personally interacted with his subjects while taking annual tours all over the empire. He listened to the grievances of people and resolved issues, punishing the wrongdoers. He abolished certain regressive taxes and improved the cultivation of lands. This brought prosperity. Infrastructure, too, saw tremendous development during his reign.

Krishnadevaraya was not just a fearless warrior and an excellent administrator, he was also a scholar. His courtiers included Telugu, Kannada, Sanskrit and Tamil poets. He had eight Telugu poets in his circle whom he called Ashtadiggajas. One of these was the famous Tenali Raman, the courtier who was known for his quick wit. The greatness of Krishnadevaraya earned him many sobriquets: Andhra Bhoja (Andhra Scholar King), Kannada Rajya Rama Ramana (Lord of the Kannada empire), Mooru Rayara Ganda (King of Three Kings) and a few more.

Man of Peace

Name: Lal Bahadur Shastri
Birth Date: 2 October 1904
Place: Mughalsarai, India
Death Date: 11 January 1966
Place: Tashkent, Uzbekistan

Delhi, the early 1960s

When he returned home late in the evening one day, Lal Bahadur Shastri, the Union Home Minister of India in the early 1960s, was surprised to find his school-going sons awake. They wanted to know why they had to go to school in a tonga (horse carriage) and not in a car like the other kids. The kids further added that they felt out of place in front of those kids, whose fathers were government officials, some of whom were in the home ministry and, in fact, worked under the Home Minister. Shastriji explained that he did not have a personal car and he could only provide his children with a government car as long as he was a minister. The day he was out of office, it would be back to the tonga for the children. The children thought switching back to the tonga after being used to a car for some time would be even worse, so they decided to continue to commute to school in the tonga.

Shastriji led honesty by example. He maintained a logbook for the official car to record its usage for private purposes. At the end of the month, he would pay back the amount corresponding to personal use to the government. Throughout his life, Shastriji was the epitome of values— he maintained the same values even when he went on to occupy the top post in India as its second prime minister.

Interestingly, Lal Bahadur Shastri dropped his surname Srivastava when in school. Shastri was not the surname of the family. In fact, he was given the title Shastri, meaning 'scholar', by Kashi Vidyapith as part of his bachelor's degree award. An informal school, Kashi Vidyapith was set up to educate young Indian activists, and this was where Shastriji completed his studies. He was an ardent freedom fighter and held many parliamentary posts after Independence before becoming India's second prime minister in 1964. His conduct in public office is a gold standard for any office bearer.

Lal Bahadur Shastri personified the ordinary Indian. He represented the aspirations and dreams of a common people who wanted to progress with a young independent nation. In short, he understood the people's language. While he was a competent minister, nobody ever thought that the mild-tempered and soft-spoken person would be the force behind India's win over the invasion of Pakistan in 1965.

At the time that Shastriji took charge, India was undergoing extreme food crisis as a newly independent country. He then directed the Planning Commission's attention towards agriculture. This change in the direction of agriculture policy led to the Green Revolution. He also helped launch the Intensive Cattle Development Programme, which later led to the White Revolution, during his short tenure as prime minister. While the former's goal was to escalate and increase agricultural coverage across the country, the latter was to increase milk production to make India the largest milk producer in the world. His slogan 'Jai Jawan, Jai Kisan', glorifying the soldiers and the farmers during the crucial war and food paucity, still echoes in the vast corridors of this country.

'There comes a time in the life of every nation when it stands at the crossroads of history and must choose which way to go. But for us, there need be no difficulty or hesitation, no looking to right or left. Our way is straight and clear—the building up of a socialist democracy at home with freedom and prosperity for all, and the maintenance of world peace and friendship with all nations.' The virtues of honesty, integrity and loyalty towards the country that Shastriji displayed at every step will forever remain unparalleled.

The Sufi Poetess

Name: Lal Ded
Place of birth: Pampore, India
Place of death: Kashmir, India

It is said that when Lal Ded's in-laws had organized a feast for the family's well-being and prosperity, some of her neighbours had teased Lal Ded, saying she should share the lavish meal with them as well. Hearing this, she had famously remarked: 'Whether they kill a ram or a sheep, Lalla will get a stone to eat,' which is a famous proverb in Kashmir to this day. Legend tells us that Lal Ded had an unhappy marriage and often didn't get to fill her stomach. Her mother-in-law used to put a stone on her plate and layer it with a thin crust of rice; to an outsider, it would appear that the plate was full. Her meditative immersion and visits to temples were viewed with suspicion and she was even accused of cheating her husband.

At twenty-six, Lal Ded decided she had had enough and left home to become a disciple of a Shaiva saint.

It is believed that Lal Ded was born during the political upheaval in the Kashmir region in the early 1300s, an era when the kingdoms were getting replaced. The last of the Hindu kings of Kashmir, Sahadeva, was displaced by a Central Asian chieftain named Zulchu, who forced locals to convert to Islam. Years later, Shah Mir took over the domain and his dynasty ruled for two centuries in the region. Lal Ded was named Lalleshwari at birth and did receive primary education. She was married off at the age of twelve and renamed Padmavati, a common ritual among Brahmins in those times. A little more than a decade later, she revolted against the atrocities inflicted by her family and walked out.

Free-spirited Lal Ded went to a saint, Sidda Srikantha, and became his disciple. After completing her learning under the guru, Lal Ded gave up clothing along with unnecessary cultural baggage and wandered as a mendicant, composing her famous *vakhs* (verses) and surviving on alms. It was not an easy life for Lal. Even the humiliations inflicted by people could not deter her from becoming a great quester and teacher.

Her vakhs, in the forms of songs and hymns, made her Kashmir's most famous poetess. They still resonate through the beautiful valley of Kashmir and are believed to be the earliest expressions of Kashmiri literature. Some scholars even consider them the foundation of the modern Kashmiri language. Her secular ethos penetrated her works. The poet Ranjit Hoskote writes in his book, 'To the outer world, Lal Ded is arguably Kashmir's best known spiritual and literary figure; within Kashmir, she has been venerated both by Hindus and Muslims for nearly seven centuries. Lal Ded was constructed differently by each community, but she was simultaneously Lallesvari or Lalla Yogini to the Hindus and Lal'arifa to the Muslims.'

Lal Ded communicated about the sorrows and the disappointments that one has to face during a lifetime in her vakhs. She also talked about the higher truth and mystic experiences. It is believed that she translated the complicated Shaiva literature, which was originally written in Sanskrit, into a common language that was accessible and understood by the masses, thus making it popular.

Lal Ded's poetry was later translated into English and titled *The Wise Sayings of Lal Ded* by George Grierson, a civil servant and the superintendent of the Linguistic Survey of India. Later, many other scholars like Pandit Anand Koul, Sir Richard Carnac Temple, Jayalal Kaul, Coleman Barks, Jaishree Kak Odin and Ranjit Hoskote also produced translations of Lal Ded's vakhs.

Lal Ded brought a bold mystic and philosophy of life to her vakhs, one of the reasons why they are considered an important part of Kashmiri folklore and literature even today.

A Voice of Change

Name: Laxmi Narayan Tripathi
Birth Date: 13 December 1978
Place: Thane, India

Laxmi Narayan was born in a boy's body, but she knew that she was a girl. While the world laughed at her effeminate mannerisms, her family always stood solidly behind her though they didn't actually realize that she was transgender.

After finishing school, Laxmi became part of Ashok Row Kavi's (LGBT activist) team working on repealing Section 377, which criminalized homosexuality. She appeared for the first press conference in this regard and spoke on camera to Zee TV. Her family was shocked to learn through TV that their child was transgender. Though there was an initial emotional drama, her family quickly accepted her as a transgender person. When asked how he accepted his child's sexuality, her father said in a BBC interview subsequently, 'If my child was handicapped, would you even ask me whether I'd have asked him to leave home? And just because his sexual orientation is different?'

Laxmi continued to live her life as a transgender person and achieved popularity through different activities. However, she often had to deal with society's intolerance. In April 2010, on the eve of delivering a TEDx talk, she was asked to leave the Mumbai Gymkhana Club on account of being transgender. Laxmi had already achieved celebrity status by then and all guests at the club walked out in solidarity. Not to be cowed down, Laxmi took the gymkhana to the Human Rights Court, demanding an apology. In 2012, she was asked to be part of the committee that was drafting the women's policy— the first time that a transgender person was included in this matter.

Her efforts, along with that of other activists, led to a landmark verdict in 2014. The Supreme Court of India ordered governments to recognize transgender as the third gender and implement the change in official documents. In addition, the courts asked entities to provide reservation quotas. It was stated that transgender people would have equal rights to adopt. An elated Laxmi stated, 'The progress of the country is dependent upon human rights of the people and . . . Supreme Court has given us those rights.' The repeal of Section 377 by the Supreme Court in 2018 was another huge success for Laxmi and other transgender people.

As expected, Laxmi's young years were not easy. She was often ridiculed and abused. 'It was the society that kept reminding me at every stage that I was different. I never felt I was different from society. I wanted to do normal things, live life normally, but people would not let me,' she says. Her family's support helped her maintain her identity and follow her passion, which was dance and theatre. They encouraged her to finish graduation from Mumbai's Mithibai College, followed by a master's degree in Bharatanatyam.

These days, Laxmi is a successful activist, choreographer, actor and motivational speaker. She has, over the years, won many hearts by being honest about her sexuality and by virtue of her activism for transgender people. 'I faced patriarchal pressures and many challenges in my evolving journey, but my faith and love in the power of the feminine and my own femininity stood by me. I have been aware of my feminine strength.'

Laxmi came out strongly in support of the movie *Laxmii*, whose main character is transgender. Sections of the media criticized the movie for its portrayal of a transgender person and even Laxmi's praise for it, but Laxmi believes the Akshay-Kiara starrer was a sensitive depiction of her community. 'Any transgender is equal to any man or woman, which comes out from the film in a very strong way,' she says.

Deccan's Moon

Name: Mah Laqa Bai
Birth Date: 7 April 1768
Place: Hyderabad, India
Death Date: August 1824
Place: Hyderabad, India

In the year 1802, Mir Nizam Ali Khan of Hyderabad held a grand celebration in his court on the occasion of Navroz (the Persian New Year) to honour soldiers and courtiers with gifts, titles and grants. Amongst the men stood a lone woman in her mid-thirties.

Chanda Bibi was exceptional by any standard, having excelled in multiple areas. Though she had started as a courtesan, Chanda grew to be an accomplished poet known for her wit. She had added warrior skills to her repertoire to join the Nizam's army and went to multiple wars, impressing everyone with her javelin throwing and archery skills. Political adviser to the Nizam, she was also known as a patron of the arts.

Navroz of the year 1802 was indeed special for her.

The Nizam conferred upon her the formal court tile 'Mah Laqa Bai', which means 'Madam Moon-faced'—a name she would be remembered by for generations to come. Additionally, the Nizam allotted her lands to collect revenue and even gave her an honorary guard and kettledrums to clear the road before her palanquin. She was a powerhouse who was recognized as high nobility by the Nizam.

Mah Laqa Bai was born to Kanwar Bai and a nobleman in 1768. However, she was raised by Kanwar Bai's eldest childless daughter Mahtab Kanwar Bai, a courtesan and companion to a Nizam's prime minister named Rukh Dawla.

Greatly influenced by her half-sister, Mah Laqa Bai learnt the art of taking pride in beauty and grace. Since Mahtab Kanwar Bai accompanied Dawla to the wars and social ceremonies, she was an influential and charismatic woman. While Mah Laqa Bai learnt articulation from her half-sister, she absorbed spirituality from her mother. The atmosphere at home was that of grandeur and prestige. She gained knowledge from poets, illustrators and historians. Her personality bloomed as she was introduced to Persian and Urdu languages, Kathak, classical music at an early age. She grew up into a refined lady who entered aristocratic circles as a dancer and a courtesan. Many were left enthralled by her dance performances and poetry recitals in *mushairas*.

In a short time, she became the star of court rituals and religious festivities. She was appointed as an omrah (high nobility acting as an adviser on state policies) in the Nizam's court. Eventually, she embraced many roles—poet, artist, musician, dancer, political adviser, warrior and religious patron. She even fought three battles dressed as a man.

Mah Laqa Bai is known to have contributed vast amounts of money towards the education of girls back in her day. She opened a cultural centre where girls could live and be trained by their tutors. She also organized a seven-day 'urs' (cultural festival) where scholars and artists were invited to exchange ideas. She was a collector of rare books and even commissioned a library. Considered the first female poet to publish her Diwan (a collection of poems), *Diwan-e-Chanda*, she was the most influential woman of eighteenth-century India.

Mah Laqa Bai not only built a cultural centre, library and stepwells, she also built a grand mausoleum for her mother at the foot of Moula Ali Hill outside Hyderabad. Beautiful gardens and fountains surrounded it. After she died in 1824, she too was buried alongside her mother in the same place.

In a time when women were not allowed to step out of their purdah, Mah Laqa Bai conquered so much. Her life continues to remain a glowing inspiration two centuries hence.

The Spice King

Name: Mahashay Dharampal Gulati
Birth Date: 27 March 1923
Place: Sialkot (present-day Pakistan)
Death Date: 3 December 2020

'Karol Bagh! Connaught Place! Paharganj! Daryaganj!' The voice of a young Dharam rang across the portico of the New Delhi railway station as the evening train pulled up to the platform. This young tongawalla was looking hopefully at the clutch of people moving out of the railway station with their luggage. 'Come *saab*, come *memsaab*, only two annas per *sawari*. Free for children.'

A family of three—a husband, wife and toddler—soon settled into the carriage of the tonga, bound for a Karol Bagh hotel. Amidst the clip-clopping of his horse Bhurav's hooves and the tinkling of his bells, Dharam gathered that the family had come to Delhi to shop for a family wedding. As Dharam dropped off the family at

213

Karol Bagh and started towards home, he reflected on the day's collections, feeling satisfied. He was doing well for a tongawalla, having been in the business for a year or so. The money from operating the tonga was enough to sustain his family on a day-to-day basis.

However, he knew he had it in him to be more successful than most of the seth passengers he ferried, like the family who had been able to travel this far just to shop. Had it not been for the vagaries of the Partition of India and Pakistan in 1947, they would have continued living in Pakistan and their family's spice business, popularly known as Deggi Mirch Wale, would have no doubt gone to newer heights.

As a tongawalla, Karol Bagh was the end point for so many of his trips. When he saw the hustle and bustle of business on the streets of this busy neighbourhood, Dharam decided he would not want to end his life as a tongawalla. He would continue his family business of making and selling quality spices here in Delhi, and Karol Bagh would be the start of his new empire. He would buy a small shop there.

MDH (Mahashian Di Hatti) started in a small wooden shop in Karol Bagh in 1948.

Mahashay Dharampal Gulati started selling spices in this shack and within a span of ten years, opened his first spice factory. A diligent worker with a sharp business sense, Dharam opened many spice factories, one after another, to become India's most popular spice brand. This gave him the title of 'The Spice King'. '*Asli masale sach sach* . . . MDH, MDH!' became a popular jingle on television and radio, in which MD Gulati played an endearing grandfather to promote his products.

From losing everything during Partition to now being a symbol of trust for his own brand, MD Gulati turned the odds in his favour through sheer hard work.

On being asked why he didn't get popular superstars to promote his masalas, he said, 'Why should I ride on their success to promote my brand? I am the man behind the success of my product, so shouldn't I be promoting it?'

Today, MDH is a household name, trusted by millions all over the world.

Dharam was not just a sharp businessman but also a good human being. Always meeting everyone with a welcoming smile, he was known as the man of all communities. Not only did he provide employment to many, he also opened many schools and hospitals for the underprivileged.

'My motivation to work is being sincere in product quality sold at affordable prices. And nearly 90 per cent of my salary goes to charity in my personal capacity,' he said in one of his interviews.

He was conferred with the Padma Bhushan for Trade and Industry on 16 March 2019.

He passed away at the age of ninety-seven, leaving behind a rich spice empire that continues to add joy to every Indian's meal.

The Writer Activist

Name: Mahasweta Devi
Birth Date: 14 January 1926
Place: Dhaka, Bangladesh
Death Date: 28 July 2016
Place: Kolkata, India

Mahasweta was born into a family of litterateurs and artists who raised her to love books, music, theatre and films. While in her twenties, she happened to read a book on Lakshmi Bai, the queen of Jhansi. The book inspired Mahasweta to pen her own tale about the great queen of the 1857 Indian uprising against the British.

Young Mahasweta was in Kolkata at the time and after writing the initial pages, she realized that something was amiss. She had torn away 300–400 pages of the draft already as the story seemed to lack spirit. She decided to go to Jhansi to understand first-hand how events unfolded in the queen's life. While in Jhansi, Mahasweta researched extensively, talking to the descendants of the queen, going through available documentation as well as dipping into the local history and oral literature. What emerged finally was a classic historical biography that was also a rich and imaginative fiction.

More importantly, Mahasweta weaved the story as a narrative of the people, including Dalit and indigenous communities. Primarily based on memory and folklore, the book was in stark contrast to the academic and upper-class interpretations of the queen's life, which earlier narratives had propagated. Mahasweta went on to become a literary stalwart of post-colonial India. 'The real history is made by ordinary people . . . in various forms of folklore, ballads, myths and legends, carried by ordinary people across generations. The reason and inspiration for my writing are those people who are exploited and used, and yet do not accept defeat. For me, the endless source of ingredients for writing is in these amazingly noble, suffering human beings,' she said.

Mahasweta Devi worked as a clerk, a teacher and a journalist before establishing herself as a writer and social activist. She wrote popular fiction adapted from folklore for children, textbooks, plays, stories and even biographies. She would base her stories on myths, legends and ballads that she had heard on her numerous travels. She also became a fierce activist, fighting for the most oppressed— the tribals of India. Her works would also comment on the atrocities that they had to face at the hands of landlords, moneylenders and the perceived 'upper caste'.

With a pen, she raised her voice against the discrimination and pathos of the tribals, the lack of education, healthcare and infrastructure in tribal areas—'I find my people still groaning under hunger, landlessness, indebtedness, and bonded labor. An anger, luminous, burning, and passionate, directed against a system that has failed to liberate my people from these horrible constraints is the only source of inspiration in all my writing.' Her writings mobilized a movement against industrialization in the rural areas and farmland grabbing by the industrial giants at throwaway prices—a reality only arresting writing is capable of achieving. Although she wrote about the struggles of oppressed communities, she never allowed her own voice to dominate theirs. Her stories always belonged to the people, only aided by her skilful writing.

Many of her works were translated into other languages too. A few of her stories were adapted into movies, like *Rudaali*, *Hazaar Chaurasi Ki Maa* and *Sangharsh*. Her list of awards and accolades is long, including the Sahitya Akademi Award, Jnanpith Award, Ramon Magsaysay Award, Padma Shri and Padma Vibhushan. In 2012, she was nominated for the Nobel Prize for Literature.

She passed away in 2016, leaving behind a legacy of 100 novels, twenty collections of short stories and a powerful story of a woman who dared to claim space for herself and her writing.

The Ace of Doubles

Name: Mahesh Bhupathi
Birth Date: 7 June 1974
Place: Chennai, India

When Mahesh was in his mother's womb, his parents would often watch tennis matches. That's as early a head start as one can take for one's passion in life, like Abhimanyu of the Mahabharata.

Mahesh's father, Krishna Bhupathi, was a tennis player who himself couldn't pursue his dreams due to a car accident. However, he was determined to make his son a tennis champion and this meant he would be a hard taskmaster through Mahesh's formative years, putting the boy through gruelling schedules of practice. Leisure, in the form of holidays or even attending birthday parties of classmates, was an unknown concept to the future tennis star as he would mostly be found on a tennis court. When he wasn't practising, Mahesh was catching up with schoolwork. Making mistakes on the court meant being yelled at and putting in extra hours to get back on track.

When he was eleven, and again when he was thirteen, Krishna took his son to Wimbledon. The boy knew then that he wanted to be on the court one day at this Mecca of tennis. All the hard work and childhood sacrifices paid off in a glorious way for Mahesh starting 1994–95, when he became India's national champion and also earned All-America honours after an exemplary career at the University of Mississippi.

Mahesh made history in 1999 when he and Leander Paes won the men's doubles title at Wimbledon, being the first Indians to do so. Bhupathi's Grand Slam success journey had already started a couple of years before when he teamed up with Rika Hiraki of Japan to win the mixed doubles title at the French Open in 1997, becoming the first Indian to win a Grand Slam title. By the time he hung up his racket, a whopping twelve Grand Slam doubles titles were under his belt—four were men's and eight mixed—a phenomenal achievement that earned him recognition as one of the most dominant doubles players in tennis history. In the case of mixed doubles, he is one of only eight players who have achieved a Career Grand Slam, winning all the four major championships—Wimbledon, French Open, US Open, and Australian Open—at least once.

Mahesh also partnered with leading women players, including Mary Pierce and Martina Hingis, during his golden run in the mixed doubles; the last two mixed doubles Grand Slam wins came while partnering with Sania Mirza.

However, his most famous liaison in the tennis world was undoubtedly with Leander. When they first hit the scene, it seemed to be a fairy-tale association, with the two hitting it off like close siblings and coming to be known as 'Lee-Hesh'. In 1997 and 1998, the magic duo won six of the eight Association of Tennis Professionals (ATP) finals that they reached. In 1999, they took their performance a notch higher by reaching the final of four Grand Slams and ended up winning two of them (Wimbledon and French Open), reaching the top rank in the ATP doubles ranking. They went on to win the French Open in 2001 as well. The pair also holds the record for the most successive Davis Cup doubles wins. Sadly, personal problems saw the full-time partnership ending, though they occasionally appeared together, including the 2004 Athens Olympics, where the duo finished fourth.

At the time of his retirement in 2016, Mahesh Bhupathi had appeared in 1000+ doubles matches. In addition to his on-court exploits, Mahesh also established International Premier Tennis League (IPTL) to promote tennis in India. He was awarded the Padma Shri in 2001 for his achievements.

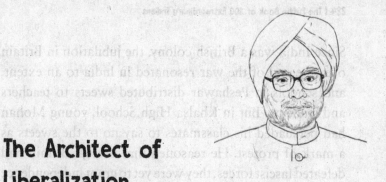

The Architect of Liberalization

Name: Manmohan Singh
Place of birth: Gah (present-day Pakistan)

Mohan was a bright student and, at thirteen, had topped his school in the common examination for Class 8 conducted across the North-West Frontier Province in British India. In fact, he had ranked third in the entire province—this was in 1945 and Mohan was studying at the Khalsa High School for Boys in Peshawar. The achievement resulted in Mohan getting extra attention from teachers and admiration from friends, family and neighbours.

In the same year, in August, World War II ended. Thanks to his habit of devouring newspapers and listening to radio news, Mohan realized that this was a seminal moment in world history. Though the war hadn't seen much action in India, the British Indian Army had fought across Africa, Italy, South-East Asia and Burma.

Since India was a British colony, the jubilation in Britain over the end of the war resonated in India to an extent, and schools in Peshawar distributed sweets to teachers and students. But in Khalsa High School, young Mohan had persuaded his classmates to say no to the sweets as a mark of protest. He reasoned that though Britain had defeated fascist forces, they were yet to grant independence to India.

This was perhaps Mohan's first brush with politics.

Forty-six years later, Mohan would be Manmohan and would formally start his political career as the Finance Minister of India and, in his maiden speech in parliament, would quote Victor Hugo, 'No power on earth can stop an idea whose time has come.' Through his liberalization measures, he would go on to rescue India from the verge of bankruptcy to one of the fastest developing economics.

Manmohan was born into a poor farmer's family. His father had to leave the village and shift to Peshawar to earn a living, leaving Manmohan behind with his grandparents. Later, during the Partition between India and Pakistan in 1947, Manmohan lost contact with his father during the migration. It was a year later that the family reunited. Manmohan matriculated from Panjab University. A brilliant student, he won a scholarship to the University of Cambridge and upon his return, he taught at Panjab University for three years. Post this, he returned to Britain as a research scholar at Oxford. Settling in a foreign land never attracted him. 'Staying in Britain after completing my D.Phil never occurred to me. I grew up at a time when there was great optimism, great enthusiasm for remaking India as a developed economy, inspired by what was happening in the Soviet Union. There was also the belief that hard work and sustained investment can transform a country in a generation.' True to this belief, he returned to India in 1969 as a professor of economics at Delhi University.

In the next few years, Manmohan joined the Ministry of Foreign Trade as an economic adviser, and slowly made his way to the post of chief economic adviser of the Ministry of Finance. Later, he accepted the position of Minister of Finance offered to him by the Narasimha Rao government.

Although diving into politics was not easy for the academician, what he perhaps lacked naturally he made up for with sheer grit and hard work. What followed then was unprecedented growth of economic liberalization in India. He revamped taxes and regulations, which resulted in the fall of inflation and growth of the economy. India got out of nuclear isolation under his leadership.

In 2004, soft-spoken 'low-decibel' politician Manmohan Singh took charge as India's first Sikh prime minister. A socialist at heart, he served the country for two terms working with a belief that 'you cannot sustain a democratic polity unless those on the lower rungs of the socio-economic ladder feel that they are partners in the processes of change.'

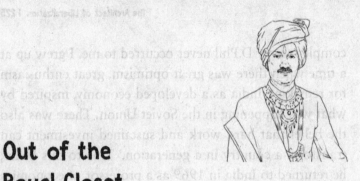

Out of the Royal Closet

Name: Manvendra Singh Gohil
Birth Date: 23 September 1965
Place: Ajmer, India

Prince Manvendra Singh Gohil knew that his interview with the Gujarati newspaper, *Divya Bhaskar*, would send shock waves in his local community and cause a rift between him and his family. But he was tired of hiding his identity from society. Aware that homosexuality was seen as taboo in India, he thought perhaps his coming out of the closet would facilitate more open discussions on gay rights. Lastly, he wanted to break the misconception that members of the royal family were always in heterosexual relationships.

But when the front-page headlines in the newspaper screamed 'The Prince of Rajpipla Declares That He's a Homosexual' on 14 March 2006, life forever changed for the prince. It was the day of Holika Dahan, and the people of the town burnt his photos in the fire. They demanded that he be stripped of the title and cast out from society, that he not be allowed to attend any public functions. His own parents subsequently disowned him through a newspaper notice that said Manvendra was involved in activities not acceptable to society. But Manvendra stayed truthful to himself.

Identifying as someone from the LGBTQIA+ community was a criminal offence back then under Section 377 of the Indian Constitution, put into effect by the archaic British law. The gist of the law states that two people could not be in a romantic relationship unless they were of two different genders, that is, a man and a woman. His coming out helped kindle the debate on homosexuality and gave hope to millions like him.

With some setbacks and lots of success, Manvendra went on to become the first openly gay prince in the world. He used his royal status to champion the rights of the LGBTQIA+ community in India and abroad.

Born as a direct descendant in a dynasty of Gujarat that was hundreds of years old, Prince Manvendra was expected to carry forward the royal legacy on his shoulders. Though he lived in a palace with hundreds of servants at his beck and call, he was unhappy. After his marriage broke, he tried to explore his sexuality.

In 2000, he started the Lakshya Trust in Gujarat to help the gay community there. Dedicated to HIV/AIDS prevention and educating the LGBTQIA+ population, the trust works towards providing decent employment to sexual minorities.

Manvendra believes that educating people about homosexuality is the only way to remove the stigma associated with it. 'It is time for us to create as many allies as possible, which I am doing myself and encouraging others to do as well. For me, an ally is a person who is not a part of the LGBTQIA+ community, yet openly supports us and accepts us. In that, we will be able to establish ourselves prominently in mainstream society. The best way to do this is through education and awareness.'

He is also the founding member of the Asia Pacific Coalition on Male Sexual Health and is an ambassador consultant of the AIDS Healthcare Foundation. He inaugurated EuroPride, a gay pride festival in Stockholm, Sweden, on 25 July 2008. Manvendra also featured in a BBC Television series, *Undercover Princes*.

Love is love, and Manvendra proudly champions that!

Magnificent Mary

Name: Mangte Chungneijang Mary Kom
Birth Date: 1 March 1983
Place: Manipur, India

Young Mary Kom had neither seen coach L. Ibomcha Singh before nor did she know that he did not appreciate being disturbed during his training sessions. Driven by what she thought was her calling and knowing that Ibomcha was the perfect guide for her first steps, she walked into the hall to ask the students about Oja (a Manipuri honorific) Ibomcha. A beefy man who Mary thought looked like Mike Tyson walked up to her and said, 'I am Sir Ibomcha. What do you want with me?' Mary said she wanted him to be her boxing coach. The coach asked who she was and asked her to wait outside till his training session was over. Mary waited and prayed that she would be accepted as a student. Oja Ibomcha finally came out and wondered why Mary wanted to join boxing. He said she was a frail girl. Pointing at her gold earrings, he remarked that she didn't look like a boxer and that the sport was for 'young boys'. Sensing the girl's disappointment at his remarks, Ibomcha inquired about her family and where she lived. Finally, he said, 'If you are really interested, you may join, but I am very strict about the routine and timing. If you can't keep up, don't join.' Mary was ecstatic—she could follow her dream now.

Mary Kom was born into a low-income family in Manipur. Her parents were tenant farmers who struggled to make ends meet. She was the eldest of four children and helped her parents in the fields, while also taking care of her siblings and pursuing her studies. She was always inclined towards sports and was an excellent athlete. However, when Manipur-born boxer, Dingko Singh, won a gold medal for India at the Asian Games, it was a turning point in Kom's life. Inspired by him, she soon took to boxing and started training in Imphal.

Though Mary's father was a wrestler when he was young, he believed that boxing was not suitable for girls. This did not deter Mary Kom and at the age of fifteen, she left home to join the Sports Academy in Imphal. The turning point in her journey was when she started training under Coach Ibomcha, whom she considers to be one of her best coaches ever. Later, she trained under Manipur state boxing coach, M. Narjit Singh. In the year 2000, Mary Kom's hard work and perseverance paid off. She won the Manipur State Boxing Championship. Then, in the year 2002, she won her first gold medal in the World Championship. After that, there was no looking back.

Mary Kom took a break from boxing in the year 2005 when she got married. In an interview, she said, 'I had to overcome a lot of hurdles and negative criticism to achieve success, especially after marriage.' However, she was determined, and nothing could stop her from doing what she loved most. She made a comeback with a vengeance. In 2012, she won the bronze medal at the Olympics and became the only woman boxer from India to achieve this feat. In 2014, she became the first Indian woman to win a gold medal at the Asian Games.

Mary Kom, also popularly known as Magnificent Mary, was the first Indian woman to win a gold medal at the Commonwealth Games in 2018. For her outstanding achievements, the government of Manipur presented her the title 'Meethoi Leima', which means 'Great Lady'. She was also awarded the Arjuna Award, Padma Shri, Rajiv Gandhi Khel Ratna Award and Padma Bhushan by the Indian government. Mary Kom started the Regional Boxing Academy, where she teaches boxing to underprivileged youngsters for free. The journey of Mary Kom is an inspiration to many. As she says, 'Each medal of mine narrates a story of struggle.'

Mary, in one of her interviews, said, 'To be a successful boxer, one must also have a strong heart. Some women are physically strong, but fail when it comes to having a strong heart. One also must have the zeal and the right fighting spirit. We work harder than men and are determined to fight with all our strength to make our nation proud. God has given me the talent and it's only because of sheer grit and hard work that I have made it so far.'

Fearless Storyteller

Name: Mira Nair
Birth Date: 15 October 1957
Place: Rourkela, India

Young Mira was part of the course in visual and environmental studies (study of visual arts including photography and filmmaking) at Harvard during the 1970s. During the summer, she went to New York and observed different theatre artists, including Ellen Stewart, Peter Brook and Andrei Serban. But Mira's most important exposure was to Elizabeth Swados, who was making a musical, *Runaways*. The musical, about the lives of children who run away from home and live on the city streets, planted the first seeds of her film *Salaam Bombay!* in Mira's subconscious, though it would be more than a decade later that the classic would release.

Post her studies, Mira created various documentaries. Some were shot in Mumbai, which she thought gave a good context to the subjects. During that period, Mira was exposed to the underbelly of the city and she came to appreciate Mumbai for what it was. Once, at a traffic junction in Mumbai, street kids surrounded her taxi, singing and blowing bubbles. Mira was attracted to the exuberance they displayed though fate hadn't been kind to them.

In the days that followed, Mira and her friend decided to make a film about them by casting actual street kids as they thought actors who hadn't come from the streets wouldn't be able to display the same authenticity of childhood and wisdom. As the word spread that a 'play' was being created with street kids, many of them turned up.

Initially, Mira focused on music and dance with the kids as part of preparatory workshops but later, when the kids were comfortable, she introduced other mature topics, including parents, gangs, making money and sex. And then, slowly, reel by reel, a classic was born. Mira made sure she put part of the 'acting fees' for the kids in fixed deposits. The film became an international sensation, winning accolades worldwide. Mira went on to create several other acclaimed movies, often mixing pluralistic themes.

Mira's romance with English literature began during her school days. Not just language, she also had a keen interest in theatre, which led her to act in several plays. In fact, before film-making, she had even thought of becoming an actor. But fate had another role for her to play. Reciting an incident, she once said that her sitar teacher had taught her a lesson that you have to choose what you want to do.

During her days at Harvard, while studying film-making, she started exploring Indian culture as a subject. She projected the same ethos in a documentary named *Jama Masjid Street Journal*, which showcased the streets of Old Delhi. What followed was a smorgasbord of documentaries and movies which gained international acclaim at film festivals in Cannes, Venice and many more.

Always fascinated by different cultures and countries, especially East Africa, she made *Mississippi Masala*, which told the story of Ugandan-born Indians living in the United States. While researching in Uganda, she was so captivated by the people and the land that some years later, she opened a training institute named Maisha Film Lab that caters to aspiring film-makers in East Africa.

In 2016, she made *Queen of Katwe*, a movie based on the story of Ugandan chess prodigy Phiona Mutesi. Mira says, 'If we don't tell our own stories, no one else will.' She believes that 'to make films, you have to have something to say. To have something to say, you have to be a student of life. And to be a student of life, you have to be feeding yourself with what life, politics, society, and your family fuels you with.' Mira's films always shifted themes because of which her film-making cannot be typecast. According to her, every film is a political act, a display of your opinion.

Apart from being a film-maker, Mira is also a social activist. She used the profits from *Salaam Bombay!* to open a trust for street children called Salaam Baalak Trust in Mumbai. She teaches film-making at Columbia University.

Awarded the Padma Bhushan, Mira Nair is a director that the world knows and loves. She brought Indian cinema to the world and believes, 'It is because my roots are strong, that I can fly.'

Numero Uno
Business Leader

Name: Mukesh Ambani
Birth Date: 19 April 1957
Place: Aden, Yemen

Mukesh was in his early twenties, at the Stanford Graduate School of Business, about to complete the 'young professionals' programme and join the World Bank, when he got a call from his industrialist father, Dhirubhai Ambani, who had established Reliance Industries Limited. Reliance was setting up a new polyester plant from scratch in Patalganga, Maharashtra. Dhirubhai asked his son if he would be interested in leading the project. Mukesh took the next flight home.

Mukesh was told that he would have to lead the project independently. His father would be there if really needed but wouldn't hold his son's hands and tell him what to do. It was also decided that Mukesh could have only one person from his father's existing organization and would need to build the rest of the team himself. Another condition was also put in place: Mukesh would need to complete the project in under two years—failing which his father would look for someone else to lead the project.

Several industry folks said that it was impossible to complete a project of such complexity in two years. Mukesh wasn't well versed with the industry yet and did not know what impossible meant. He gave the project everything he had, and it was completed on schedule. With this first milestone behind him, Mukesh built upon the foundations that his father had laid. Turning each stone over, within the next four decades, Mukesh made Reliance a trailblazer of a company that ventured into uncharted territory. It became a company that made a habit of achieving the impossible. Even today, Mukesh believes that polyester laid the foundation of the vast empire standing today, 'We have a whole host of infrastructure portfolios today, but it all began with Papa's vision for polyester. It was the lifeline for Reliance.'

Reliance Industries has shown tremendous growth under the leadership of Mukesh Ambani—from manufacturing polyester yarn to petrochemicals to oil and gas exploration, he has steamrolled Reliance Group into almost everything. To ensure Reliance could become self-sufficient, free from dependency on other suppliers, he even implemented backward integration (develop one's own supply chain) early in his career.

A visionary like his father, Mukesh Ambani created the world's largest petroleum refinery in Jamnagar, Gujarat, in the late 1990s. This catapulted Jamnagar as the refining hub of the world.

Today, retail and communications play a vital role in day-to-day life. Following this thought, Mukesh single-handedly revolutionized the telecom sector by launching Reliance Jio in 2016. He made it possible even for people below the poverty line in India to afford a cell phone. This resulted in creating a global record in customer acquisition for Jio, the reliance digital service. Its Wi-Fi network caters to several segments, such as education and healthcare, security and financial services, government-citizen interfaces and entertainment.

A relentless businessman, Mukesh Ambani is also a man of values. He cares not just for his family and friends but also for those who work for him and work with him. Over the years, this soft-spoken man has built a trustworthy persona and as a result, millions of people have faith in his ability to lead the nation's growth. He is an astute businessman who believes in knowing everything about each pie he puts his fingers into.

Mukesh Ambani lives in a twenty-seven-storey building in Mumbai named Antilia, which is said to be the most expensive home in the world. He is believed to be a risk-taker and believes, 'Dance to your own music and take some risks in life because it is often the risk-taker who changes the course of history, who innovates, who creates something the world desperately needs and contributes to the well-being of millions of lives.'

Pioneer Writer

Name: Mulk Raj Anand
Birth Date: 12 December 1905
Place: Peshawar (present-day Pakistan)
Death Date: 28 September 2004
Place: Pune, India

Perched on a rock in his neighbourhood in Peshawar, little Anand was cheering the elder boys on as they played kabbadi. He was included neither as a player nor as a referee as he was quite young, but that didn't deter him from screaming his head off as a cheerleader.

Anand was wholly absorbed in the game in front of him when a Dalit sweeper's boy overpowered a boy from an upper caste. The upper-caste boy was livid, calling it a foul and saying that an underprivileged had no right to touch and 'pollute' him. The argument between them grew to a point where the upper-caste boy hurled a stone at the Dalit, who evaded it by ducking. Instead, the stone hit Anand on the back of his head. Blood spurted from the little boy's head as he cried in pain and fear.

While most of the boys ran away, the Dalit boy quickly picked Anand up in his arms to comfort him. The commotion brought Anand's mother to the door of their house and when she saw the underprivileged boy holding her son, she was furious. She cursed him for touching her son. The boy had tears in his eyes as he handed Anand over to his mother. In his pain, Anand was baffled that the Dalit had to bear the flak for helping him as any human would do. And at such a young age, Anand understood how poorly people of the lower castes were treated.

The incident left the deepest impression on Mulk Raj Anand. He grew up and became one of the torchbearers of Indian writing in English in the twentieth century. Even today, he is admired for his realistic portrayal of the prevailing caste system.

Mulk Raj Anand completed his schooling in Amritsar before moving to London, where he pursued graduation and a PhD in philosophy. After completing his doctorate, he stayed back in Britain. His first novel, titled *Untouchable*, was published in 1935 and to date remains one of the groundbreaking works that portrays the reality of the caste system in India. E.M. Forster, a notable English novelist, had written the introduction for the novel.

Post the release of his first novel, Anand continued writing many books and stories revolving around social issues that plagued Indian society. These included works like *The Village, Across the Black Waters, Coolie, The Sword and the Sickle* and many more. Through his works, he brought alive Indian characters in English literature. In fact, it is said that Anand's works paved the way for authors like Vikram Seth and Salman Rushdie.

Interestingly, Mahatma Gandhi greatly influenced Anand. After his return to India in 1945, Anand joined the Indian Freedom Movement. Anand went back to England in 1948, and in 1952, received the International Peace Prize. He became the head of the cultural division of the World Peace Council. He travelled worldwide, giving lectures on the issue of cultural self-awareness among nations, and made friends with people like George Orwell and Pablo Picasso. In the meantime, he continued writing thought-provoking novels.

He once said, 'To me the idea of political freedom in India was always only a stepping stone towards that larger freedom of the whole world. As Gandhi used to say, "Let all the winds of the world blow in; let us open our doors and windows and only see that we are not swept off our feet by these winds." There is so much knowledge . . . coming from all parts of the world that so much more interchange, a new consciousness, must take place . . . this means that prejudices against other ways of thought must stop. My idea of co-existence is co-discovery.'

In a time when the social realities of British India prevailed across the country, he attempted to capture the same in the language of the British Raj. Deeply committed to the cause of social change, Anand left behind a legacy that echoes values of social justice, secularism and humanism. He was conferred with the Padma Bhushan in 1967 and the Sahitya Akademi Award in 1971.

Daring Cartographer

Name: Nain Singh Rawat
Birth Date: 21 October 1830
Place: Milam, India
Death Date: 1 February 1882
Place: Moradabad, India

It was 30 March 1865, and Nain Singh and his cousin Mani were on an undercover mission of mapping Tibet. They had been waiting at the Nepal–Tibet border for two days now, and felt a bit apprehensive.

The Chinese customs officer could let them enter only if the governor of Kyirong town explicitly allowed them. He had sent a messenger to the governor seeking his permission. When they had arrived at the point two days earlier, the cousins had cooked up a story that they belonged to the Bushahari tribe (who were permitted to enter Tibet freely). Since they looked like Bushaharis and could speak Tibetan fluently, they could get till here.

They had told the guard that the purpose of their visit was to purchase horses and also pay homage to the shrine in Lhasa. The cousins had cleared the luggage search. Thankfully, the sextants and other cartography instruments hidden in their luggage were not caught. Finally, the officer summoned them. The cousins' hopes were dashed as the letter from the governor of Kyirong denied them entry into Tibet.

In his letter, the governor had said that this route through Kyirong wasn't a regular route to Tibet and if they were indeed Bushaharis, they would have crossed through Lake Mansarovar. Despondent, Nain and Mani turned back. Even the advance toll of Rs 5 that they had deposited two days earlier with the officer was only partly refunded.

But the bigger worry was that months of their training on preparing maps seemed to have gone to waste. Their hope of mapping Tibet was ruined. However, Nain Singh didn't give up that easily. If not this one, he would find some other route into Tibet to complete his mission.

During the nineteenth century, Europe was interested in the geographical vastness of central Asia. There was a curiosity to understand the people and customs of the region—knowledge was essential. However, Europeans couldn't always enter wherever they liked.

Nain and Mani were therefore employed by the British authorities to map Tibet with the intention of acquiring it. However, their journey had not been easy.

Born into a poor family, Nain's father was driven out of the community due to misconduct. Nain lost both his parents at an early age. Getting a little help from one of his relatives, he tried his hand at animal husbandry for a couple of years but was unsuccessful. He was also married by that time. However, his financial situation remained terrible.

Then he heard that his cousin Mani was working as a surveyor for the Schlagintweit brothers (German geographers). Mani got him a job. Once in the circle, Nain outshone others by displaying his skills at using cartography instruments. The German brothers respected Nain's intelligence and even invited him to accompany them to London for three years to help them prepare details.

However, perhaps out of jealousy, Mani influenced Nain's decision, and he did not go.

Opportunity knocked again a couple of years later when Nain was chosen for a two-year training for exploring lands. Nain had learnt cartography from Captain Thomas George Montgomerie at the Great Trigonometrical Survey of India in Dehradun. He learnt how to use a compass, barometer, sextant and how to follow stars. He was also taught undercover surveying techniques, for example, using 108 holy bead strings with only 100 beads to count steps, hiding information in prayer wheels and much more.

Within ten years, Nain had completed three big expeditions—estimating the altitude and position of

Lhasa, exploring western Tibet and exploring the northern route to Lhasa. Apart from putting Lhasa on the map, he accurately located the source of the Brahmaputra River.

Calculating distance through the steps he had walked on vast terrains, accomplishing greatness at the risk of his life, he was awarded the Royal Geographic Society's Patron's Medal for his work. To honour his explorations of the Himalayan region, a postage stamp featuring him was released in 2004.

Nain Singh was a fascinating man, bringing accurate surveys with meagre resources as he explored uncharted territories.

The Wonder Woman of Banking

Name: Naina Lal Kidwai
Place of birth: New Delhi, India

Three years after her graduation, Naina studied chartered accountancy and also interned with PricewaterhouseCoopers (PwC). Being ambitious, Naina's heart was set on getting an MBA degree from a prestigious university in the United States.

This was in 1980—when in India only a handful of the students made it to the US to study as there were no direct flights. It wasn't easy to speak uninterrupted on the phone either. On top of that, the cost of education was exorbitant for an MBA in the US. So, Naina's extended family firmly opposed this idea. Her uncles even said that she should not waste her parents' money and time and must consider getting married.

However, her resolve only grew stronger with each additional ounce of resistance. She was determined to break the glass ceiling that women had to face, not just by getting into Harvard but by making the journey of her life worthwhile. With her parents' support, Naina flew to Harvard in September 1980 and, in 1982, graduated from Harvard Business School as the first-ever Indian woman to do so. She returned to India and continued flying high for decades to come, as a revered banker and iconic corporate leader. In her own words, Naina 'challenged two institutional myths: gender and age.'

She was not only the first Indian woman to graduate from Harvard but also one of the first three women employed by PwC, the first woman to head the foreign bank HSBC in India and the first female president of the Federation of Indian Chambers of Commerce and Industry (FICCI).

Naina has been instrumental in bringing the Indian financial market at par with international standards by becoming a member of working committees set up by Reserve Bank of India. From critically analysing modern banking systems to helping establish the National Stock Exchange of India, Naina's contribution to financial sector is monumental.

Taking inspiration from her parents, she maintains that her father's position and integrity as the CEO of a leading Indian insurance company helped her decide that she wanted a corporate career. Her mother urged her to look beyond academics and excel in extracurricular activities. So she played basketball and badminton, learnt piano, took part in public speaking events and in her college, she was the first president of the student's union to introduce cultural and academic intercollegiate festivals.

Naina was a leader in the corporate world. She strove to earn the loyalty and trust of people who worked with her. As Narayana Murthy, founder of Infosys and past board member at HSBC, puts it, 'Naina is a leader who made each one of her colleagues feel an inch taller. She made them more confident, more aspiring.'

A philanthropist, she believes in giving back to the society.

Naina is actively involved with the NGOs (Grassroots Trading Network for Women and Self-Employed Women's Association) that work for the empowerment of underprivileged women. An example of this is her setting up a business school for rural women in Satara, Maharashtra. She believes, 'No economy can thrive or even survive by ignoring the contributions of women . . . Every time I see a group of women going door to door delivering the petticoats that they had sewed on machines purchased on credit or see a woman vegetable vendor use her mobile phone to monitor prices prevailing in the mandi before she sells her goods, I know we are headed in the right direction.'

She is also associated with sanitation drives (founding chair of the India Sanitation Coalition), and environmental conservation programmes (founder of Water Mission at

FICCI and governing council member of The Energy and Resources Institute). She underlines the importance of sustainable growth, the challenges involved and ways of achieving it in her book *Survive or Sink*.

Quoting George Bernard Shaw in her book, Naina states, 'You see things; and you say, "Why?" But I dream things that never were; and I say, "Why not?"' In the year 2000, she was declared the 'Third Most Powerful Businesswoman' in Asia by the *Fortune* magazine. In 2002, *TIME* magazine selected her as one of the '15 Most-Promising Young Executives'.

Naina is a true inspiration and a wonder woman.

A Scientist Who Powered India's Mars Mission

Name: Nandini Harinath

'Space: the final frontier. These are the voyages of the Starship Enterprise. Its five-year mission: to explore strange new worlds, to seek out new life and new civilizations, to boldly go where no man has gone before.'

As Captain Kirk's voice heralded another episode of *Star Trek*, the cult science fiction series that aired on Doordarshan in the 1980s, little Nandini settled down in front of the television with her parents. She loved watching Captain Kirk's adventures and his famous crew—Mr Spock, Dr McCoy and Scotty, amongst others—as they travelled to the far corners of the galaxy, encountering different forms of alien life, some hostile, some friendly.

While Nandini had no idea what she wanted to be once she grew up, her fascination for *Star Trek* was indeed a harbinger of what fate had in store for her.

Born to philomaths, she grew up to be a respected rocket scientist at the Indian Space Research Organisation (ISRO) after graduating from IIT Madras in electronics engineering as the gold medallist in her batch.

The date 24 September 2014 stands out in the Indian space exploration story as the day Mangalyaan was successfully propelled into the orbit of Mars. As the deputy operations director of the famous Mangalyaan Mission (Mars Orbiter Mission), Nandini, along with her team, successfully steered the Mars Orbiter. With a budget no bigger than that of a Hollywood film, India became the first nation to reach Mars's orbit in its maiden attempt. Interestingly, till today, only 40 per cent of the missions to Mars have been successful.

'It was the turning point not just for ISRO but for India too. The success of Mangalyaan put us on the global map,' says Nandini.

For Nandini, this day had arrived after almost two decades of service in ISRO, during which she was a part of fourteen different space projects. A beautiful moment was captured with the team of women scientists at ISRO, dressed in saris and wearing flowers in their hair as they patted each other's backs.

Nandini worked long hours at the ISRO office while also juggling all the responsibilities she was expected to fulfil at home. While ISRO interacted with the public over social media, the team worked under high pressure and short deadlines.

'We spent many sleepless nights. We encountered lots of problems as we progressed, in the design as well as in the mission. But coming up with quick solutions and innovations was the key,' she said in one of the interviews.

Nandini believes women must claim the field of science and maths. She says, 'It's a myth that women aren't interested in math and science. Our society is plagued with a cultural myth that girls are inherently uncomfortable with computing, math and science. My take on this is that it is not true.' In a field traditionally recognized as male-dominated, Nandini believes that she would like to be known as a scientist, not a woman scientist.

Her contribution to Mangalyaan not only brought newfound respect for India as a leader in space travel but also inspired the younger generation to dream big and work hard.

Well, metaphorically and at least in India's context, Nandini would 'boldly go where no man has gone before', echoing the iconic lines from her favourite show, *Star Trek*.

The Fastest Indian Behind the Wheel

Name: Narain Karthikeyan
Birth Date: 14 January 1977
Place: Coimbatore, India

On a moderately hot weekend in February 1992, Indian motor sport fans flocked to a glitzy new racing strip in Sriperumbudur, Chennai, to witness the national-level competition, which ran for just two weekends a year. The track had come into existence in 1990 and was a significant upgrade from the earlier racetrack, which was a repurposed World War II airstrip. The edition in 1992 was a Formula Maruti (FISSME) race, which, along with the regulars, saw a puny fifteen-year-old boy—the son of a former national rally champion—making his debut. Narain Karthikeyan finished on the podium that day in his first professional outing, stunning experienced competitors. But nobody except Narain himself had imagined that the boy would go on to become India's first Formula 1 driver.

Narain was born in an environment of motor sport. His hometown, Coimbatore, has always been India's motor sport hub. To add to it, his father had been a successful rally driver in the 1970s and 1980s. At the young age of ten, Narain had decided that he wanted to be a Formula 1 driver. However, his parents did not take him very seriously then, thinking that the lack of motor racing opportunities in India would make it a passing fad.

But his success in the Sriperumbudur race ahead of other well-known Indian racers made his parents think that perhaps the boy could have a career in this field. However, there was neither any infrastructure for race training in India at the time, nor were there any trainers. 'When I decided to become a racer, there were no training academies, nor could any person teach me the same efficiently. However, I stayed focused and kept working hard till I achieved my dream,' Narain said in one of his interviews.

Narain soon found himself at the Winfield Racing School in France, pitted against the finest racers in Europe and America. At the school, Narain was the only Asian and while he could fit in with the rest, he did notice that the others were physically much fitter. However, Narain believed in his potential and went on to win a scholarship by securing first rank in his batch. There was no looking back from that point. Driven by a strong will to succeed, Narain braved challenge after challenge to achieve higher and higher goals and one day emerged as the first Indian Formula 1 driver.

Karthikeyan has a list of firsts in the Indian racing scenario. He was the first Indian to win a trophy at the British Formula Ford Championship Winter Series in Europe in the early 1990s. He entered the British Formula 3 Championship in 1998 and the Formula Nippon F3000 Championship in 2001. The same year, he created history by becoming the first Indian ever to test drive the Formula 1 car. Four years later, in 2005, Narain was crowned the first Indian to race in Formula 1. This debut brought a massive change in Narain on a personal level. Typically, Formula 1 racers are required to be incredibly fit to handle the mean machines. Extraordinary stamina and lower back, leg and arm strength are essentials for the racers. Until then, Narain had been working out regularly. But now, after racing Formula 1, he had to amplify his fitness regime.

Through extreme grit and determination and against all odds, Narain competed in Formula 1, A1 GP, NASCAR, LMS, the 24 Hours of Le Mans, Superleague Formula, Auto GP and Japanese Super Formula Championship races in the last twenty-five years. He won several races, secured pole positions many times and did the fastest laps and created records.

Ratan Tata invited Karthikeyan to share his expert opinion on developing new cars at Tata Motors in 2010. He, to date, works closely with the research and development team of Tata Motors.

Karthikeyan established Speed NK Racing Academy in 2006, where talented youngsters are trained in motor sport. Through his passion and commitment, he has challenged the thought that motor racing is only a rich man's hobby. He believes that following one's passion and making the right moves at the right time is the key to success.

The Father of Linguistics

Name: Panini
Birth Date: Between the sixth and fourth century BCE
Place: North-western India

Legend has it that several centuries before Christ, somewhere in north-western India, a little boy called Panini was studying at a *gurukul* under a renowned guru. The guru wasn't happy with Panini's progress at studies. Though the guru gave personal attention and the boy showed great dedication towards learning, he however could still not retain anything. The guru's frustration at the student's inability to learn grew to such an extent that he took out a stick to whack the boy on his palm one day. However, looking at the boy's palm, the guru stopped. When Panini asked why he was spared, the guru said there was no 'education line' on the palm, which meant the boy would grow up illiterate; he could stop coming to the gurukul and learn other skills.

After gleaning where the education line on the palm was supposed to be, Panini left the place. The guru was stunned when the young student returned a few days later with blood oozing from his hand; using a sharp instrument, the boy had 'carved' an education line on his right palm. Panini asked his teacher if he could become a scholar now. Moved by the boy's thirst for knowledge, the guru said he would redouble his efforts to teach Panini. The boy with the artificial education line went on to become a celebrated linguist who framed the rules for the mother of many Indian languages—Sanskrit.

Panini's work is titled *Ashtadhyayi* (*aṣṭādhyāyī*). It is divided into eight chapters, further divided into quarter chapters. These chapters define and explain the description of word formation, word order system and Sanskrit grammar syntax. The document also clearly states the differences between spoken Sanskrit and the one used in religious texts. It lucidly explains how to interpret and read Sanskrit text. The perfection of this document has helped scholars follow the rules mentioned in it for centuries now. Modern linguists worldwide study composition and do further research on languages. It has been reiterated that Panini's Sanskrit grammar has inspired many European languages. Ferdinand de Saussure, the father of modern structural linguistics, is believed to have been highly influenced by Panini's work. Many scholars have compared *Ashtadhyayi* to the Turing machine, a mathematical model considered one of the bases for modern artificial intelligence in machines.

G.G. Joseph, in *The Crest of the Peacock*, states that '[Sanskrit's] potential for scientific use was greatly enhanced as a result of the thorough systematization of its grammar by Panini. On the basis of just under 4000 sutras [rules expressed as aphorisms], he built virtually the whole structure of the Sanskrit language, whose general "shape" hardly changed for the next two thousand years.'

To say that Panini, the great Sanskrit grammarian, contributed to many linguistic, mathematical and scientific innovations is not an exaggeration.

The Gentle Tiger

Name: Prakash Padukone
Birth Date: 10 June 1955
Place: Bengaluru, India

Bengaluru, the early 1960s

Prakash, all of seven, was excited as he entered the badminton court in Bengaluru to compete for the Karnataka State Junior Championship. The state junior championship was his first badminton highlight. Unfortunately for him, however, even a seven-year-old had to compete in the common category for under eighteen. His opponent that day was a player much older and stronger. It was no surprise that Prakash was quickly overcome by his opponent. Heartbroken, the little boy cried at his loss. In his defeat, however, Prakash discovered that he had a hunger to win. With determination and focus, he returned two years later to win the junior state title at the age of nine. Victory after victory, Prakash worked his way to becoming a legendary name in badminton.

As a child, he had learnt badminton from his father, who was part of the first state association for badminton and used to play primarily for fitness. Prakash had practised in unusual places, like wedding halls in Malleswaram, due to inadequate badminton infrastructure in Bengaluru in those days. Not just that, he had watched and learnt from state-level players who practised in the same hall. Prakash also kept practising on his own along with his father. 'My father taught me the fundamentals. After that, I picked up the game by watching other players. Basically, I am a self-made player who came up by following the trial-and-error method.' Hard work paid off and at the age of eighteen, he championed both state and national levels.

Five years later, he bagged the gold medal at the 1978 Commonwealth Games in Edmonton, Canada. The subsequent year saw him winning the Danish Open, Swedish Open and the prestigious All England Championship, successfully dethroning the Chinese and Indonesian players, placing India on the world map of badminton. He trained in Denmark to fine-tune his talent. Years later, in one of his interviews, he said, 'Champions don't wait for things to happen; they find their own ways to win, fair and square. They don't wait for success to come to them; they go after success. That's the hallmark.

A true fighting spirit and intense passion is a crucial learning from sport.'

Post his retirement, in 1991, Prakash opened a badminton academy in Bengaluru, which coaches young badminton players who are groomed based on their talent. His mentees include P. Gopichand, Sayali Gokhale and Ashwini Ponnappa. He also served as the chairman of the Badminton Association of India and the coach of the Indian national badminton team for three years, from 1993 to 1996.

A few years later, he co-founded Olympic Gold Quest with billiards maestro Geet Sethi. The mission was to 'support Indian athletes in winning Olympic medals'. The association supports sportspersons of nine disciplines—badminton, shooting, athletics, boxing, wrestling, archery, swimming, table tennis and weightlifting. This Arjuna and Padma Shri winner is not just a champion but a creator of champions. He believes, 'Parents should try to find out activities a child is interested in and support them. It is important not to impose the views of the parents on the child . . .'

Father of Statistics in India

Name: Prasanta Chandra Mahalanobis
Birth Date: 29 June 1893
Place: Kolkata, India
Death Date: 28 June 1972
Place: Kolkata, India

Growing up, Prasanta was not too bothered with reading textbooks in the syllabus and passing exams in school. Instead, he would immerse himself in books on topics that interested him that were not necessarily in the syllabus. He was known for his analytical mind and would readily sacrifice the conventional for the original. Perhaps he stretched his quest to be original a bit too far while preparing for his intermediate exams in Presidency College. As per the rules, students were expected to get minimum passing marks in all subjects in the qualifying test conducted by the college to be eligible for the final examination. Prasanta appeared for the English test and wrote two essays. However, he did not appear for the remaining tests. Any other student would have been disqualified from appearing for the final examination for this misdemeanour. But in Prasanta's case, the college principal was bowled over by the quality of the two essays and allowed this whimsical student to appear for the final examination.

The genius boy, Prasanta Chandra Mahalanobis went on to become the father of modern statistics in India. He founded the Indian Statistical Institute, devised methods for large-scale surveys and shaped the Planning Commission of India. He is easily a pioneer who brought the concept of planned governance to India.

The Brahmo Samaj influenced Prasanta's family, and therefore his upbringing was in a liberal environment. He studied at Presidency College after school, followed by King's College in Cambridge. It was here that he met the famous mathematician Srinivasa Ramanujan and built a long-lasting friendship with him.

After his return to India, Prasanta taught physics at Presidency College for three decades. Along with his teaching, he also held the post of meteorologist at the Alipore Observatory in Kolkata for a couple of years.

He believed in the aim of statistics, which is to give adequate knowledge of reality with the help of numbers and numerical analysis. It was this belief that brought together a group of enthusiasts informally at the Statistical Laboratory in Presidency College, which later expanded into the Indian Statistical Institute (ISI), an institute to facilitate research and learning of statistics. He also launched *Sankhya: The Indian Journal of Statistics*, which is still in circulation, and covers research on theoretical statistics, probability and applied statistics.

In 1955, he joined the Planning Commission and served there for twelve years. Many believe that the industrialization in India was the result of the second Five-Year Plan (1956–1961), which relied on Mahalanobis's mathematical description of the Indian economy; it later came to be known as the Mahalanobis model.

His notable achievements include devising the 'Mahalanobis distance' that compares two datasets— an integral part of the modern fields of data science and artificial intelligence (in clustering and classification techniques). He also developed a statistical method called fractile graphical analysis, which compares the socio- economic conditions of different segments of society. His data analysis on the floods in Odisha became one of the bases for the construction of the Hirakud Dam on the Mahanadi River—the first major multipurpose river valley project of independent India. He contributed to the agricultural field, too, by introducing a method for estimating crop yields.

The imprints of Mahalonobis's genius run deep in the annals of history. His effective surveys and data- based policy decisions for human welfare and national development are still relevant.

Prasanta was conferred with many national and international honours and awards, including the Fellow of the Royal Society, London (1945) and the Padma Vibhushan (1968).

India honours Mahalonobis's contribution to the field of statistics and mathematics on his birthday, 29 June, as National Statistics Day.

Beauty with a Purpose

Name: Priyanka Chopra
Birth Date: 18 July 1982
Place: Jamshedpur, India

Priyanka was twelve that summer and was looking forward to her upcoming school vacation. However, at night, she found out she would need to first accompany her parents (both doctors in the Indian Army) to a medical camp in a nearby village. This would mean a delay in the vacation and she tried to resist, but her parents wouldn't listen. She soon found herself in the medical camp helping distribute medications to the poor.

At the camp, she observed that while parents in the villages were bringing their boys with medical issues to the camp, only a few girls were turning up. Even after much persuasion, only a few parents and husbands in the village brought their girls or wives for medical examination. While driving back once the medical camp ended, Priyanka asked her parents why the girls in the village were not allowed to seek medical help easily for their problems. Her parents explained that in India, many parents didn't want their girls to be seen by doctors because discovering a medical issue would impact the chances of finding a groom.

Priyanka compared the plight of the rural girls with herself, who had all the freedom that she wanted, and wondered at the disparity. The trip to the medical camp changed Priyanka by solidifying the humanitarian values that her parents had already introduced her to. She understood that being privileged also meant being responsible. As she achieved unimaginable fame and became an icon of beauty and entertainment, Priyanka remained a firm advocate for underprivileged children, particularly girls. She continues to make a difference in myriads of lives through her charitable acts.

Due to her father's postings, Priyanka had travelled across the length and breadth of India in her childhood years. In an interview, she said that this movement between cities made her adaptable, which helps her even today.

She learnt classical music and choral singing, honing her singing talent during her teenage years in the United States. However, after facing racism at school, she returned to Bareilly in India and completed her senior secondary schooling there. Priyanka learnt to command a strong sense of self-worth, having experienced bullying at a young age. In an interview, she said, 'I was told to have an opinion in a room that disagreed with me. I was always encouraged to have a voice.'

Growing up, Priyanka wanted to become an aeronautical engineer, but instead she garnered fame by winning the Miss World title at the age of seventeen.

Winning the title also paved her way into the film industry. What followed was a string of blockbuster movies over the years. She received critical and widespread acclaim for several movies like *7 Khoon Maaf*, *Barfi!* and *Fashion*. She was once described as 'one of the most powerful actresses in the current lot and someone who doesn't shy away from experimenting with roles within the realms of popular cinema'.

Globally, Priyanka made a mark and broke glass ceilings for women to trust their talent and abilities. She entered the international stage by acting in the American network drama series named *Quantico*, for which she also became the first South Asian actress to win a People's Choice Award. Since then, she has been a force to reckon with.

An all-rounder, Priyanka stands tall today as an actor, singer and film producer. She is a two-time National Award winner for her performances and was also awarded the Padma Shri in 2016. She is the only Indian actor to have a statue in four Madame Tussauds locations around the world.

At a young age, she navigated the mysterious world of entertainment and ascended to the top with great hard work and determination. She is also known for her philanthropic activities. Her support for underprivileged children, mostly girls, through her foundation, The Priyanka Chopra Foundation for Health and Education, has been relentless.

A champion of gender quality, she believes that women, especially young girls, should be able to decide whatever they want to do and whoever they want to be, instead of having someone else decide it for them or impose it on them. Leading by example, Priyanka Chopra is truly an inspiration.

Hargila Baideu (Stork Sister)

Name: Purnima Devi Barman
Birth Date: 24 November 1980
Place: Assam, India

Purnima was in her late twenties in 2009 and had completed her master's degree in zoology. Aspiring to be an academician, she was pursuing her PhD and was in Dadara, a village in Kamrup, Assam, for the fieldwork.

One day, she received a call about a tree being cut down. Upon reaching the scene, she was aghast to find that a person had chopped down a kadam tree in his backyard, which had nine nests of the greater adjutant stork ('hargila' in Assamese), an endangered scavenging bird of the region. The nine baby birds in those nests had fallen to the ground, some dead and some alive.

Purnima plucked up courage and asked the man why he had cut down the tree. She was yelled at in return. Soon, the person's neighbours joined him and mocked

Purnima. Later, she understood that people thought that an 'ugly-looking' almost five-foot-tall hargila was a bad omen, a disease-carrying creature that needed to be got rid of.

When Purnima requested them to help her rescue the birds, they teased her further, commenting that she was interested in eating them. While walking back home that day, Purnima realized that a PhD was pointless when she couldn't motivate the villagers to protect the hargila. She decided to put her PhD on hold and adopt a new mission for her life: to protect the endangered stork whose numbers were dwindling by educating and motivating the villagers.

At 6 a.m. the next day, armed with perseverance, she started her mission by meeting people and educating them and has never looked back since.

Purnima had often seen hargilas flocking her grandmother's paddy fields during her childhood days. She could see their numbers dwindling while growing up. After finishing her master's, Purnima joined Aaranyak, a non-government organization for biodiversity conservation, where she formally started the stork conservation project.

At the time, there were less than thirty nests left in the region. She started working with the villagers and led crusades that weaved the local culture and traditions to conserve the endangered birds. She actively involved village women in campaigns and formed 'Hargila Army', an all-female conservation group. The delegates of the group educate locals about the importance of storks, organize competitions, arrange festivities and offer scholarships for the children of the villagers who participate in stork conservation.

Purnima directs her army to motivate people to do everything to save the birds, from cooking competitions to skits and plays to getting stork motifs weaved into clothes. Taking time out of her busy schedule, she frequently teaches children how to rescue and rehabilitate a hargila. Over the years, she has successfully created a local ecosystem that fully supports the existence of hargilas. Her efforts have brought a lot of recognition to the cause.

She was the recipient of the highest civilian award for Indian women—the Nari Shakti Puraskar—in 2017. She was also awarded the prestigious Whitley Award (also known as the Green Oscar) and the UNDP India Biodiversity Award (2016), among many others. Several bodies worldwide recognize her contribution towards the conservation of birds and are willing to provide aid for her cause.

The Celebrated Economist

Name: Raghuram Rajan
Birth Date: 3 February 1963
Place: Bhopal, India

In August 2005, the world's leading central bankers were attending an annual symposium in Jackson Hole, Wyoming, USA. Amidst different speeches by the dignitaries, there was one by the young chief economist of the International Monetary Fund (IMF), Raghuram Rajan, who presented a paper titled 'Has Financial Development Made the World Riskier?' Raghu, who was only forty-two, highlighted what he viewed as hidden dangers in the financial system and concluded that the world was indeed riskier due to financial development. The paper was met with much scepticism by those at the conference as well as other leading economic voices of the time.

However, all those opposing Raghu's warning were proved wrong within two years when the US financial crisis began to unfold, hitting its peak in 2008. When this happened, everyone acknowledged Raghu's speech as prescient, and he was extensively interviewed for the American documentary *Inside Job* on the financial crisis in the late 2000s. One of the few to have effectively straddled the vastly different worlds of central banking, academics and policymaking, Raghuram Rajan became truly known to Indians when he took over as governor of the Reserve Bank of India (RBI) in 2013. A year earlier, Rajan was appointed the chief economic adviser to India's Ministry of Finance.

Thanks to his public persona, a role which till then was confined to the top echelons of government and industry was suddenly all over the media. People from different walks of life sat up and took notice of the new RBI governor.

Raghu had been a professor at the University of Chicago and had to take a leave of absence from the university during his tenure as the governor of RBI from 2013–2016. He had a formidable task in front of him after taking over as the RBI head: the Indian rupee was weakening and inflation had skyrocketed to double digits, amongst other problems, which saw a crisis of confidence in the Indian economy. Raghu spearheaded strategic new initiatives and ventured into unexplored territories to bring the economy back on track and restore investor confidence.

By the time he left in 2016 to re-join academics, inflation was cut to half of what it was when he had started, the rupee was under control and stock markets had gone up. But most importantly, India had seen an RBI governor who did not hesitate to communicate with the masses. Being from an academic background and having extensive knowledge of his subject area, Raghu made several speeches on the state of the economy and the steps being taken, which further endeared him to the common man. For the first time in India's history, there was much debate and interest about his continuation for a second term in 2016, which did not happen.

Raghuram Rajan excelled in education right from childhood. After schooling, he graduated from IIT Delhi with the Director's Gold Medal for all-round performance, and went to do his MBA at another stellar institution— IIM, Ahmedabad. After finishing his MBA course, Raghu pursued his PhD from MIT Sloan School of Management and received a doctoral degree.

Raghu has a list of several national and international awards and recognitions in the area of economics to his credit. TIME magazine included him in the '100 most influential people in the world', in 2016. He has penned several books, of which *Fault Lines: How Hidden Fractures Still Threaten the World Economy* won the

Financial Times and Goldman Sachs Book of the Year Award in 2010.

One of the finest minds in the world, Raghuram Rajan is a true genius who continues to make India proud.

The Warrior of the Fourth Estate

Name: Ramnath Goenka
Birth Date: 22 April 1904
Place: Darbhanga, India
Death Date: 5 October 1991
Place: Mumbai, India

On the night of 25 June 1975, the newspaper offices located on Bahadur Shah Zafar Marg in Delhi experienced a sudden power cut. Simultaneously, the government began raiding presses across the country, stopping printing and seizing bundles of newspapers. These actions against the press made complete sense once Prime Minister Indira Gandhi announced the following day that the President had proclaimed Emergency (a twenty-one-month period when all freedom of speech and action were cancelled) due to 'imminent security threats' to the country.

Once the Emergency under Article 352 of the Constitution was declared, the constitutional rights of citizens were suspended, and the press freedom was curbed. For the next two days, no major newspaper in the country was allowed to publish. When publication resumed on 28 June 1975, the *Indian Express*, headed by Ramnath Goenka, carried an apology on its front page for the two-day gap in circulation and reported about the mass arrests that had taken place. However, there was no editorial published in the paper and the space was left blank, representing the censorship imposed by the government as part of the Emergency. Other newspapers soon followed suit and started carrying blank editorials as a metaphor for censorship.

This unique form of protest by the *Indian Express* is remembered even today—nearly half a century later.

Goenka faced government backlash in the following days due to his tough stance against the Emergency, but he did not give up and continued to fight. When asked later why he didn't buckle, Goenka said, 'I had two options: to listen to the dictates of my heart or my purse. I chose to listen to the heart.'

Ramnath Goenka, the patriarch of the press, was born into an ordinary family of traders. He was mostly self-taught and believed in following indigenous practices. He spent his early years working for his uncles in Kolkata and Chennai. After learning the ropes of the business in Chennai for ten years, astute Ramnath acquired the loss-stricken Madras edition of the *Free Press Journal*. However, it was in 1936 that he established the *Indian Express*, challenging the British Raj. His newspaper became a mouthpiece of protest against the British rule in India. Later, he acquired several regional publications, including the *Dinamani*, the *Andhra Prabha* and the *Kannada Prabha*.

He was a freedom fighter and an industrialist. A follower of Mahatma Gandhi, Ramnath Goenka renounced material things early in life. His only passion was walking and reading books. Never having many friends, he was a loner, not close to even his own family. Following a simple lifestyle, he could not tolerate any kind of waste. Even when he could afford the best things, he travelled in economy class and never stayed in five-star hotels.

'Fear should never enter the mind of a newspaper owner. He should pay any price that the occasion demands . . . newspaper owners should care for the people and the country. Politicians and governments come and go. The newspapers are there to stay,' he said.

Never restraining his journalists, he was fearless where the truth was concerned. By the mid-1970s, his newspaper empire covered the whole country. He was a man who respected even those with whom he disagreed. But, above all, far-sighted Ramnath made a lasting contribution to journalism in India.

The Writer of History

Name: Romila Thapar
Birth Date: 30 November 1931
Place: Lucknow, India

Romila belonged to a generation that came of age along with India's independence in 1947. As someone preparing to go to college, she would wonder about what kind of society Indians were going to build, like many of her age. A related question was what is the actual Indian identity—who are we?

This search for the roots of the Indian identity attracted her to the earliest history of India.

Around that time, her father, an army doctor, visited a museum in Chennai during a tour of south India. Impressed by the Chola (one of the longest-ruling dynasties in the world's history) exhibits of the museum, he carried loads of books on iconography, classical sculpture and other books on Hindu religion back to Pune, where his family stayed. While reading the books, he wanted to discuss the subject with someone and hence it was decided that Romila would be the one giving him company since her mother was not keen and her siblings were out studying in other places.

Initially, Romila thought it was a terrible chore as she could be out doing so many wonderful things instead of reading those vast tomes. But left with little choice, she read the books for nearly six months to give her father company. At the end of those six months, she registered somewhere in her subconscious that perhaps the answers to the real Indian identity lay in looking at that very early period of Indian history.

A few years later, when she was anxious to go abroad after completing her education, Romila's father gave her a choice: he could either finance her education in London for two years or give her a dowry, but not both. Without batting an eyelid, Romila chose education. Today, she is one of the greatest Indian historians—the only one from India to have won the Kluge Prize, the Nobel equivalent for humanities and social sciences.

Like all army children, Romila's early life was nomadic. She was born in Lucknow. She and her siblings attended schools in various cities, wherever her father, Lieutenant-General Daya Ram Thapar, was posted. She completed her schooling the same year India got its independence, in 1947. She later graduated in English literature (from Panjab University) and then double-graduated in Indian history (from the University of London). She also obtained a doctorate in Indian history from the same university.

After finishing her studies, she got offers from all over the world to teach Indian history. However, she chose to return to India and teach in her homeland. She worked as a lecturer at various universities across India, including Kurukshetra University, Delhi University and Jawaharlal Nehru University. She has authored several books on the history of India in which she has objectively explored the rich past of India. Thapar also created a curriculum for history at the post-graduate level, filled with intellectually vibrant discussions that are open to all ideas. In a conversation with Karwaan: The Heritage Exploration Initiative, Prof. Thapar said, 'with every branch of knowledge, it is essential to realize that you have to ask questions. That you have to question the existing knowledge and unless you question the existing knowledge, you cannot go any further.'

Over these years as a resilient historian, activist and feminist, she has amplified her research from understanding empires and cultures to how history has been written and perceived. Most recently, her research has been about the relationship of the past and the present along with the history of dissent in India. Romila Thapar lives in Delhi and is often spotted purchasing books in old and new bookshops. True to the historian's craft, she is still found asking questions relentlessly.

Snake Man of India

Name: Romulus Whitaker
Birth Date: 23 May 1943
Place: New York City, the United States of America

Four-year-old Romulus had a great fascination for bugs and other creepy-crawlies, and liked chasing butterflies. Sometimes, he would get stung by bees, but that was a small price to pay for all the fun he had in the countryside near New York. He would upturn rocks to see what was underneath them, often discovering unusual insects. So one day, in Hoosick, New York, where his family lived, he moved yet another rock expecting to find something interesting. He was in for a surprise! Something wriggled out—a milk snake.

Rom was elated at this discovery and ran home with the snake to show it to his mother. 'It's beautiful,' said his mother and added that they could keep it at home. She knew that the snakes in that area were non-venomous and that even if the snake had bitten Rom, nothing would have happened. However, for a parent to support a child going after snakes at such an age was remarkable. By his mid-teens, Rom had his own pet python.

Thanks to all the encouragement and support from his mother, Rom pursued his passion to become a renowned herpetologist and wildlife conservationist. 'I was lucky my mother encouraged me and bought me my first book on snakes (*The Boy's Book of Snakes* and later *Snakes of the World* by Raymond Ditmars),' he once said.

Romulus spent his early childhood in New York, before his family shifted to Bombay. He continued his education at Kodaikanal International School in Tamil Nadu. It was his endless roaming through the hills that further pushed his interest in wildlife. He completed his studies in the US and briefly served in the US Army too.

Post his army duties, he joined the Miami Serpentarium, where he learnt about venom. He returned to India to continue his research on snakes and established the first snake park in India—the Chennai Snake Park in 1972. The park was also an endeavour to save the Irula tribe (known for their expertise in catching snakes) by providing them with legal livelihood. From illegal snake traders, they became snake-protectors, who, through a cooperative, did the work of extracting snake venom to produce antivenom.

A few years later, he became instrumental in establishing the Madras Crocodile Bank Trust and Centre for Herpetology. It breeds and conserves reptiles such as crocodiles, snakes, turtles and lizards. In 1996, he made a wildlife documentary, *The King and I*, for the National Geographic Channel, for which he received the Emmy Award for Outstanding News and Documentary Program Achievement in 1998.

In 2005, Romulus won the prestigious Whitley Award for conservation initiatives. He used the project funding that he received as the prize money to set up the Agumbe Rainforest Research Station in Karnataka to enable the study of king cobras and their habitats.

On being asked if he actually wore a boa coiled through his hair, he replied, 'Yes, I guess I was a pretty strange sight, a wild-haired hippy snake man with a three-foot-long sand boa tangled in my hair as I rode around on my motorcycle; it was all good for publicity though, and there were a lot of good spin-offs, including early support from the World Wildlife Fund and a couple of local and international awards and recognition for pioneering work in the subject.'

To honour his outstanding work in the field, two Indian species are named after him: the Indian boa, *Eryx whitakeri*, and the krait, *Bungarus romulusi*. Among many awards, he received the Padma Shri in 2018.

A Hindu Lady

Name: Rukhmabai Raut
Birth Date: 22 November 1864
Place: Mumbai, India

Twenty-two-year-old Rukhmabai waited with bated breath in a courtroom in Mumbai for the judge to deliver the verdict. She hoped for a favourable verdict— not being forced to live with Bhikaji, to whom she was married at eleven years of age.

Rukhmabai was a victim of child marriage, prevalent in colonial India. Bhikaji was a nineteen-year-old fellow with whom she had refused to live. She had managed to live away from him for eleven years, thanks to her determination and timely support from her stepfather, Dr Sakharam Arjun. Sakharam had helped her get legal help, as a result of which the court had given a judgement in the same year, which said that child brides like her could not be forced to stay with someone.

The judgement received a lot of criticism in the newspapers and the case had come up for retrial in

1886. Rukhmabai was least prepared for this verdict. The judge said that she should either go live with her husband or face six months of imprisonment. Rukhmabai stood her ground and said she was ready to go to jail than obey the judgement. The prison sentence was thankfully not enforced.

As the case was contested, newspapers were flooded with articles by someone called 'A Hindu Lady'. It was found that Rukhmabai used the pseudonym 'A Hindu Lady' and wrote letters to the *Times of India* in 1885. In one of the letters, she wrote, 'Sir, I am one of those unfortunate Hindu women whose hard lot it is to suffer the unnameable miseries entailed by the custom of early marriage. This wicked practice has destroyed the happiness of my life. It comes between me and that thing which I prize above all others—study and mental cultivation.'

Subsequently, Rukhmabai also wrote to Queen Victoria (as India was a British colony at the time) requesting for a change of Hindu law of marriages. In her letter, she requested the queen to bring 'change into the books on Hindu law that marriages performed before the age of twenty in boys and fifteen in girls shall not be considered legal in the eyes of the law if brought before the court.'

It is said that the queen did intervene in her case and she overruled the court's verdict.

To Rukhmabai's delight, her husband Bhikaji accepted monetary compensation and agreed to dissolve the marriage in 1888. But more importantly, Rukhmabai's case paved the way for the Age of Consent Act, 1891, which changed the age of consent for girls from ten to twelve years. The court proceedings were covered by newspapers in as far as London and America.

Free from the clutches of a pointless marriage, Rukhmabai went on to pursue her passion, i.e., studying medicine. Her education was funded and assisted by many eminent personalities of the time, including Dr Edith Pechey (one of the first women doctors of the United Kingdom). With sheer grit and determination, she made her way to the London School of Medicine for Women in 1889. Later, she came back to India and joined a hospital in Surat, where she served for the next thirty-five years.

Rukhmabai was one of the first practising women doctors in British India. Her defiance against the marriage she hadn't chosen and her thirst to become a doctor were both unthinkable in that era. Yet, she pursued relentlessly and the blood, sweat, tears and pain endured by her became instrumental in reshaping modern Indian society.

She practised medicine till her retirement in 1929, post which she remained active in foundations working for women's rights education till her death in 1955, at the age of ninety. Rukhmabai Raut's fierce battle against atrocities towards women is unparalleled even today.

Bharatanatyam Revivalist

Name: Rukmini Devi Arundale
Birth Date: 29 February 1904
Place: Madurai, India
Death Date: 24 February 1986
Place: Chennai, India

Rukmini Devi sat in her house in Adyar, Chennai, when she received a call from the then prime minister, Morarji Desai, with whom she had a good equation. The year was 1977, and as an animal rights activist, she had influenced Morarji Desai to ban the export of rhesus monkeys for laboratory tests.

On the call, the prime minister asked her if she would consent to be the President and she politely refused.

Later, when asked why, she explained, 'I like to go about barefoot. How could I have done that in Rashtrapati Bhavan? I detest arms and armaments. How could I have moved about with an AdC bearing guns in front of me and another behind me? And also as a committed vegetarian how could I have served meat to guests from abroad who cannot do without it . . .? Besides my life is bound up with Kalakshetra, the Theosophical Society, Chennai. Delhi is . . . another universe . . .'

It is said that if this successful dancer, choreographer and activist had agreed at the time, she would have been elected as the President of India unanimously. But her refusal showed the strength of her character in being committed to the performing arts industry and animal welfare.

Interestingly, Rukmini didn't learn Sadhir (later named Bharatanatyam) initially, as it was considered a vulgar dance form, performed only by devadasis at that time. Stigma and social stereotypes were associated with the dance. In fact, her journey as a dancer began on a ship when she learnt to dance from one of Anna Pavlova's (famous Russian ballerina) leading solo dancers, Cleo Nordi. Anna motivated her to explore Indian dance forms, especially Sadhir, which later led to Rukmini's efforts to revive it.

Rukmini was exposed to music, culture and theatre at an early age. Her father, Neelkanta Shastri, was a follower of the theosophical movement (bridging the gap between the eastern and western worlds) and her mother was a music lover. The atmosphere at home was liberal and progressive. She shocked the conservative society by marrying a British man, Dr George Arundale, who was also a theosophist. They travelled around the world, meeting interesting people and propagating theosophical thought.

She understood the value of a school for dance. So, in 1936, Rukmini, along with her husband, set up Kalakshetra—an institution that became synonymous with nourishing the performing arts. She approached not only experts of dance but also great musicians and scholars of her time who could compose music. Kalakshetra's salient feature was having open-air classrooms, an eco-friendly ambience where everyone could enjoy proximity with nature.

Rukmini not just brought respect and recognition to Sadhir, she renamed it Bharatanatyam, one of the most artistic Indian dance forms known today.

Apart from being a Bharatanatyam dancer, she was also an animal rights advocate. When asked how she became an activist, she said, 'I was standing one day on a railway platform, waiting for my train when I felt my sari being tugged by someone. I turned around and it was no 'someone' but a monkey, a caged monkey, pulling at my sari to ask me to help it get out of that trap . . . I felt that the monkey had given me a task, a mission.'

After being the first Indian woman to be nominated as a member of the Rajya Sabha in 1952, she worked towards releasing the Prevention of Cruelty to Animals Act and establishing the Animal Welfare Board of India. She was the first chairperson (1962) of the Animal Welfare Board of India.

Rukmini was also instrumental in preserving the ancient Indian textile printing technique using a pen called Kalamkari. The Kalamkari Centre was established at Kalakshetra to revitalize the ancient Indian craft of textile printing, which was later recognized as an Institute of National Importance.

The list of awards and honours conferred on Rukmini Devi is long—the Padma Bhushan (1956), Sangeet Natak Akademi Award (1957), Prani Mitra (1968), to name a few.

Rukmini Devi, the woman behind the revival of Bharatanatyam, broke the shackles of caste and community to renew the splendour of performing arts.

The Great Army General

Name: Sam Manekshaw
Birth Date: 3 April 1914
Place: Amritsar, India
Death Date: 27 June 2008
Place: Wellington, India

On 28 April 1971, the Indian Cabinet, under the leadership of Prime Minister Indira Gandhi, met in New Delhi to discuss the Indian response to the throes of a civil war in East Pakistan. The Pakistan military had killed thousands of Bengali protestors, creating a humanitarian crisis; more than ten million refugees had fled into India, causing an enormous burden on the border states of Assam, Tripura and West Bengal.

All attempts at diplomacy had failed. As the last resort, the prime minister and the Cabinet asked the army chief to launch a military attack on East Pakistan to bring the situation under control. However, much to the political

297

leadership's surprise, the army chief Sam Manekshaw refused to launch an attack at that point since the Indian Army was not yet prepared for a war.

He would require time to mobilize formations to the operational locations along with continuous logistical support, which would mean arranging for aircrafts, trains and trucks. It was the time of crop harvest in Punjab and suddenly diverting trains for military operations would mean food shortage in the country. Also, the Border Roads Organisation (BRO) would be needed to build roads to forward locations for non-stop backups. Lastly, monsoon was round the corner and East Pakistan would be marshy, making it easy for the opponents to stop the Indian Army. Though the prime minister hadn't liked this blunt refusal by the army chief, she understood the importance of planning the attack.

After months of careful preparation, Indian forces marched into East Pakistan, liberating it from Pakistani occupation. East Pakistan was reborn as Bangladesh on 16 December 1971. Remembered famously for resisting the political pressure, Sam Manekshaw was one of the chief architects of India's 1971 victory against Pakistan. His frank response ultimately paved the way for a glorious victory, making Manekshaw arguably the greatest general of the Indian armed forces.

Sam belonged to the first batch, called 'The Pioneers', of Indian Military Academy, set up in 1932. He showed his courage in several wars: World War II, the Indo-

Pakistan War of 1947 over the princely state of Jammu and Kashmir, the Sino-Indian War of 1962, the Indo-Pakistan War of 1965 and the Bangladesh Liberation War in 1971. He served in both the British Indian Army and the Indian Army after Independence.

He consistently climbed ranks in the army, from being a cadet to lieutenant colonel to brigadier to chief of army staff to finally, India's first field marshal—the highest attainable rank in the Indian Army. Earning these ranks was not an easy task. Sam was called Sam Bahadur for his fearless nature and outspokenness. He was an astute planner, strategist and administrator. It was these qualities that brought him success in battles he fought in when he served in the Indian army.

Nevertheless, time and again, he showed his humane side. In his radio message to Pakistani troops in the 1971 war, he said, 'Why waste lives? Don't you want to go home and be with your children? Do not lose time; there is no disgrace in laying down your arms to a soldier. We will give you the treatment befitting a soldier.'

Recipient of the prestigious Padma Vibhushan, Padma Bhushan and Military Cross Awards, Field Marshal Sam Manekshaw was not just a soldier but one of the builders of the very foundation of the Indian Army.

The Man Who Revived Microsoft

Name: Satya Nadella
Birth Date: 19 August 1967
Place: Hyderabad, India

Satya, a bright and young computer science engineer in his mid-twenties, waited for his next round of interviews on the premises of Microsoft in the United States. It had been a long, gruelling day—he was being interviewed by different engineering professionals who tested Satya's skills and resilience. The next round was with an up-and-coming manager Richard Tait. Satya tried to predict whether it would be an engineering problem to be solved on a whiteboard or a complex coding scenario to explain. But, to his surprise, Richard's question had nothing to do with technology or engineering.

'Imagine you see a baby lying in the street and the baby is crying. What would you do?' he asked Satya and replied by saying that he would call 911 (a number used to call emergency services in the US).

Richard put an arm around the young engineer and said, 'You need some empathy, man. If a baby is lying on the street crying, pick up the baby.' Eventually, Satya got the job and started a flourishing career with Microsoft. But Tait's words remained etched in his mind.

Little did Satya know at the time of the meeting with Richard that he would soon be learning empathy in a profoundly personal way via the birth of his first child Zain. Due to damage caused by asphyxia while in the womb, Zain was born with severe cerebral palsy; he would require a wheelchair throughout his life and would be heavily dependent on his parents for support as a special child. The same empathy that he developed for his child became a key pillar of Satya's leadership style that took Microsoft to unprecedented heights.

'I discovered Buddha did not set out to find a world religion. He set out to understand why one suffers. I learnt that only through living life's ups and downs can you develop empathy; that in order to not suffer, or at least not suffer so much, one must become comfortable with impermanence,' Satya believes.

At a Stanford GSB event, Nadella said, 'My father was a Marxist economist and civil servant. He looked at my grades and was amazed someone could be so bad! But he always said, "It's a marathon. You'll catch up." My mother's only question to me was "Are you happy?"'

He was a curious child and loved history, like his father. The only thing his parents wished for him was intellectual engagement and a balanced life.

Needless to say, he didn't disappoint them.

He studied electrical engineering at Manipal Institute of Technology and did his post-graduation from the University of Wisconsin-Milwaukee. While working full-time at Microsoft, he completed his MBA from the University of Chicago.

After a short stint at Sun Microsystems, he joined Microsoft in 1992 and is serving the company till now. He rose through the ranks, and today, Satya Nadella is the chairman and chief executive officer of Microsoft. Said to have rebuilt Microsoft since 2014, Nadella is only the second person—the first being Microsoft's co-founder Bill Gates—to hold the positions of chairman and CEO at the same time.

He also co-wrote *Hit Refresh: The Quest to Rediscover Microsoft's Soul and Imagine a Better Future for Everyone* and pledged the royalties he received from the book to non-profit organizations. A global icon, ranked by premium magazines such as *Time* and *Forbes*, he believes, 'We need to be insatiable in our desire to learn.'

Nadella wanted to be a professional cricketer when he was young, and still uses analogies from the sport to deal with real-life situations. Even though he did not become a cricketer, he has certainly hit multiple global sixers in the field of tech and innovation.

The 'Boson' Man

Name: Satyendra Nath Bose
Birth Date: 1 January 1894
Place: Kolkata, India
Death Date: 4 February 1974
Place: Kolkata, India

Young Satyendra Nath Bose was an aspiring scientist and worried about his future. He had always wanted to travel to Europe but had not got an opportunity. He was working at the University of Dhaka (now in Bangladesh) but learnt he would need to return to Kolkata due to a conflict between the government of India and the provincial government of Bengal. The conflict had also resulted in funds being cut off for the university. Though faced with uncertainty about his future, Bose persevered and wrote his famous technical paper on Planck's law. The paper derived Planck's law without reference to classical electrodynamics, and this ultimately led to the prediction of the Bose–Einstein condensate, a new state of

303

matter that was actually discovered decades later in 1995. He sent the paper for publication to the *Philosophical Magazine*, which, to his disappointment, rejected his paper. As a second attempt, Bose sent his paper to Albert Einstein—the world-renowned German physicist.

Along with the article, he enclosed a letter requesting Einstein to get the paper published in a German magazine if Einstein saw any merit in Bose's paper. He ended the letter with, 'Though a complete stranger to you, I do not feel any hesitation in making such a request. Because we are all your pupils though profiting only by your teachings through your writings.'

Bose's excitement knew no bounds when Einstein's reply arrived in the form of a postcard on 2 July 1924: 'I have translated your paper and given it to *Zeitschrift für Physik* for publication. It signifies an important step forward and pleases me very much.'

Einstein's postcard served as a lottery ticket for Bose. The postcard enabled a two-year study leave in Europe for Bose with a good stipend, family allowance and a sumptuous travel allowance. In addition, the German consulate issued him a visa without charging a fee, all thanks to the postcard!

The period in Europe enabled Bose to deepen his understanding of theoretical physics, eventually leading to the development of the groundbreaking theory of the Bose–Einstein condensate for the study of fundamental particles.

Bose was seen as a gifted child from a young age. Highly influenced by the Swadeshi movement, Bose took admission in Presidency College in 1909. Despite having an interest in languages and humanities, Bose decided to pursue science with the vision of making India self-sufficient. Equipped with nationalistic ideals, he lent support to the Swadeshi movement in his own ways—donating money for the movement, providing shelter to the revolutionaries and teaching kids at night school.

Despite completing his master's in 1915, Bose found it hard to get a job. An opportunity arose when the University of Calcutta introduced a separate segment for advanced courses and basic research. Bose was called and asked to learn and teach Einstein's theory of relativity. The problem was that all the available technical books were in German; therefore, Bose learnt German first! Such was his dedication towards learning.

By 1919, Bose, along with his friend and colleague Saha, had translated many research papers of modern physics into English. Two years later, he joined Dacca University, where he taught thermodynamics and Maxwell's theory of electromagnetism. He became instrumental in establishing new courses, laboratories and dedicated departments at the campus. It was during these times that he wrote his famous paper, which eventually paved his way to Europe.

After two years in Europe, he returned to the University of Dhaka as the head of the Department of Physics and introduced experimentation and practical learning, the importance of which he had learnt during his stay in Paris and Berlin. He established research centres for X-ray and wireless technologies, magnetic properties of matter and Raman Spectra.

Bose was a polymath and a polyglot; he loved to discuss various subjects, 'There would be a continuous stream of visitors to his room, and Satyendranath would get involved with their academic problems for hours. It could be any branch of physics, chemistry, history, hieroglyphs or indeed any other subject under the sun. He was engaged in creating a culture of intellectual discourse,' wrote his contemporary Partha Ghosh.

After the Partition, Bose settled in Kolkata and continued his nuclear physics and organic chemistry research at the University of Kolkata. In 1956, he was nominated for the Nobel Prize in Physics for his contribution to Bose–Einstein statistics. Boson, a term for subatomic particles, was named after him.

India's First Female Teacher

Name: Savitribai Phule
Birth Date: 3 January 1831
Place: Naigon village, India
Death Date: 10 March 1897
Place: Kartarpur (present-day Pakistan)

Young Savitri in her late teens stepped out of her house, like on any other day, determined to reach school. No, she wasn't a student. Rather, Savitri was already a teacher and headmistress at the new school for lower-caste girls. It was a school she had established with her husband, Jyotirao, in Pune.

At a time when education was not accessible to all, Savitri's intentions had attracted the upper-caste society's ire. When orthodox norms opposed the education of girls and people of lower castes, Savitri pioneered the right to education movement. Men would hurl abuses and, when she didn't stop, would throw stones at her. This would be

307

followed by a lump of dung to spoil her saree so that she had to turn back. But even this could not deter her spirit, and she began to carry an extra saree with her.

Sending girls to school at that time was simply unheard of, so Savitribai was illiterate when she was married to Jyotirao at ten years of age. Her husband, who was thirteen at the time, urged her to study and educated her at home. Later, he trained Savitribai to be a teacher. She went on to be India's first female teacher and headmistress.

Savitribai, along with her husband and a friend, believed that the right to education was essential to reform society. Therefore, they opened the country's first school for women back in 1848 at Bhide Wada, Pune. Savitribai was only seventeen at that time. The fearless couple dedicated their lives to the empowerment of lower castes, and the abolishment of discrimination and untouchability.

Savitribai initiated a movement that gave women and marginalized communities an equal position in society. Through her passionate struggle, along with Jyotirao, she fought against infanticide, dowry and child marriage. In an environment where speaking up was punishable, Savitribai paved way for women to exercise their fundamental rights.

Despite all odds and opposition from the people of the upper castes, Savitribai Phule and her husband opened eighteen schools for girls' education. The University of

Pune was renamed Savitribai Phule Pune University in the year 2015, to honour the revolutionary woman who championed the cause of equality, education and freedom in nineteenth-century India.

Her birthdate, 3 January, is celebrated as Savitri Utsav in Maharashtra as an homage to an extraordinary life.

Savitribai Phule is recognized as India's first woman teacher and headmistress, her story illustrates courage of conviction. Not only did she lead by example but also by her words:

> Go, Get Education
> Be self-reliant, be industrious
> Work—gather wisdom and riches,
> All gets lost without knowledge
> We become animal without wisdom,
> Sit idle no more, go, get education

(An excerpt from her poem 'Go, Get Education')

Powerhouse Performer

Name: Smita Patil
Birth Date: 17 October 1955
Place: Pune, India
Death Date: 13 December 1986
Place: Mumbai, India

A movie titled *Manthan* was being filmed in a village near Rajkot, Gujarat in the mid-1970s. A bunch of college kids arrived on their bicycles from Rajkot. They had heard about the film unit from Mumbai and had come to catch a glimpse of the shooting. When they didn't find any well-known stars amongst the film's cast, the boys were disappointed. Shyam Benegal, the film director, then overheard one of the boys asking in whispers, 'Who is the heroine of this film?' Someone then pointed at one of the women sitting in a group in the shade of a nearby tree. The boy who asked the question regarded the woman briefly and said, 'She can't be the heroine. She's from this village. How could she be the heroine?' The woman sitting there was Smita Patil. When not facing the camera, Smita blended effortlessly into the surroundings without any airs, like an ordinary person. But the moment she was in front of the camera, she used to turn into a spontaneous powerhouse of performance.

Smita Patil was born in Pune, Maharashtra, to the freedom fighter turned politician, Shivajirao Girdhar Patil, and nurse mother, Vidyatai Patil, who was also involved in social work. Right from childhood, Smita was compassionate and emotional and stubborn. Perhaps it was this combination that made her a great actress later on. Fond of acting from an early age, she often participated in plays during her childhood. The environment at home supported freedom of expression and perhaps that made Smita a confident speaker.

At the time when Shyam Benegal (director and screenwriter) spotted her, she was working as a newsreader at Doordarshan's Marathi channel. It was considered an unusual casting since Patil was dark-skinned. Benegal said in an interview, 'With Smita, no one would think that she'd make a film star . . . because in India you have this bias against darker skin. It is ridiculous but that's the way it is. We are one of the most colour-conscious people in the world.'

The dusky beauty then forayed into the film industry, which was ruled by fair-skin, with ease. Remarks made on her dark complexion never made Smita less confident about her talent. In fact, it became her tool to portray the girl next door, somebody with whom people could relate. Patil was inclined towards small-budget films, strong female protagonists and storylines that served a social cause.

The portrayal of feminism became synonymous with Smita Patil in those days. 'There are two types of rebels. One variety makes a huge ruckus about the manner in which they change the order of things, while the other kind is the silent ones whose actions end up making the loudest of sounds. Smita Patil belonged to the latter and in her roles millions of women found an icon mirroring their own trials, joys and struggles and a search for an identity,' notes an article.

In her short film career, she worked with stalwarts like Govind Nihalani, Satyajit Ray, Mrinal Sen, Naseeruddin Shah and many more. She starred in films like *Manthan*, *Bhumika* and *Arth*.

Ketan Mehta's *Mirch Masala* was her last film, which was released posthumously. In the movie, she played the role of an aggressive and intelligent village woman who worked as a spice worker and broke the stereotype portrayal of village women as innocent, naïve and delicate in Indian cinema. It was even voted as one of the twenty-five greatest performances of Indian film in the centenary year of Indian cinema. The government of India released a stamp in her honour to mark 100 years of cinema in 2013.

Along with National Awards, she was also awarded the Padma Shri in 1985. Though untrained, Smita Patil had an exceptional instinct, for what she achieved in her brief acting career takes a lifetime for many others to achieve. Her legacy of work left a remarkable imprint on the fabric of Indian cinema.

Innovator Extraordinaire

Name: Sonam Wangchuk
Birth Date: 1 September 1966
Place: Alchi, India

This was in the late 1980s in Ladakh.

Sonam was nearing the end of his first year of engineering in REC (now NIT), Srinagar. It was time to choose a specific branch in which he would graduate. Sonam was keen on choosing mechanical engineering as his specialization. When he mentioned this to his father, his reply was unexpected, 'Son, you should choose civil engineering instead, which has better job prospects in Ladakh. You can even make more money with civil than mechanical.' Sonam insisted that he only wanted to take up mechanical. The disagreement grew and Sonam's father made it clear that taking up mechanical would mean no support from his father's side to complete his degree. Despite the daunting prospect of self-financing the remaining three years of his education, Sonam stood his ground and walked out of his home. He knew he could teach science and maths to school students to earn money. He utilized the winter break to set up a low-cost coaching centre in Ladakh, and in two months, Sonam had saved enough to finance the remaining three years of his education. Post his engineering, too, he continued working in the field of education.

Born and brought up in Ladakh, Sonam always wanted to reform the local school system. Therefore, he founded the Students' Educational and Cultural Movement of Ladakh (SECMOL) in 1988. The school campus is like a mini eco-village where students and staff cohabit and embrace eco-friendly ways of living. While studies are experiential in nature, social and traditional knowledge is shared between all. Everyone is a learner and a teacher there. Sonam's vision is to elevate young Ladakhis from disadvantaged backgrounds with skills and knowledge so that they could sustain and grow in the fast-developing region. 'Don't blame the child for forgetting lessons; make the lessons unforgettable,' he says.

Calling Sonam only an educationist would not be correct. He is an inventor, a reformist and an environmentalist too. During the dry periods in Ladakh, the farmers face a scarcity of water. Sonam not only understood their problem but also developed a method that could preserve the winter ice. He invented conical structures that looked like Buddhist stupas to preserve ice. He called them ice stupas, which melt and provide water to the region in the summer months. For this work, he became the recipient of the Rolex Award for Enterprise 2016 in the United States of America. The idea became so popular that the president of a Swiss municipality invited Sonam and his team to build ice stupas in the Swiss Alps.

In the same year, Sonam launched another project called FarmStays Ladakh. The idea is to urge tourists to stay with local families to experience the true essence of the region and support the local community.

Sonam's latest invention in 2021 is for Indian soldiers posted in the harsh, high-altitude, cold mountains of Ladakh. He designed unique portable tents that are solar-heated and can accommodate ten people at a time. These will provide comfortable shelter to soldiers and conserve the environment from the burning of kerosene, which is what is normally used to keep warm.

Sonam Wangchuk is a diligent environmental conservationist, inventor, educator and activist who has been granted several awards, including the Ramon Magsaysay Award in 2018, the UNESCO Chair for Earthen Architecture for India in 2014, the 'Green Teacher' Award by *Sanctuary Asia* magazine in 2005 and many more.

Mathematical Genius

Name: Srinivasa Ramanujan
Birth Date: 22 December 1887
Place: Erode, India
Death Date: 26 April 1920
Place: Kumbakonam, India

Since childhood, Ramanujan was fascinated with numbers and had started challenging his teachers when he was in the third form (roughly class 7 in today's day) in school. One day, the math teacher, while explaining division, explained that any number divided by itself was one and gave an example of dividing three fruits among three people, which would give each of them one fruit. Further, the teacher said, dividing a thousand fruits among thousand people would yield the same result—one fruit per person. Ramanujan asked the teacher, 'But is zero divided by zero also one? If no fruits are divided among no one, will each still get one?' We do not know the teacher's exact reaction but it's not hard to imagine that he would have been stumped at the question; zero by zero is 'indeterminate' as per mathematical principles. A preteen boy of those times conceiving the thought signalled towards a natural genius who would one day go into uncharted realms of mathematics. Much later in his life, while hospitalized in England for what was believed to be tuberculosis, the British mathematician G.H. Hardy visited Ramanujan. Hardy had arrived in a taxi with the number 1729 and upon meeting Ramanujan in the hospital room, remarked that it was a rather dull number. 'No, Hardy,' Ramanujan said, 'it is a very interesting number. It is the smallest number expressible as the sum of two positive cubes in two different ways.' The genius was, of course, referring to the fact that 1729 is $10^3 + 9^3$ as well as $12^3 + 1^3$. The number later came to be known as the Hardy–Ramanujan number.

It is hard to believe that Ramanujan had no formal training in mathematics, but it's true! He showed exemplary results in primary school, and by the age of eleven, he had already become a child prodigy. At thirteen, he was discovering mathematical theorems on his own. He came across a book *A Synopsis of Elementary Results in Pure and Applied Mathematics*, G.S. Carr's collection of 5000 theorems, at the age of sixteen. It is believed that this book was what deeply influenced the genius.

After completing school, Ramanujan earned a scholarship to attend Government Arts College,

Kumbakonam. However, he lost it as he failed all the subjects but maths since he refused to attempt them! Later, he failed his Fellow of Arts exam too due to a similar reason—he solved only those questions that appealed to him. Years later, he was offered the post of research scholar at the University of Madras due to his astonishing work in the field of mathematics. Believed to be puzzles, his equations and theorems would baffle renowned mathematicians, who often thought of him as a fraud. There was scepticism around his work as he recorded only the results and not how he reached them. It was later deduced that this was because paper was quite expensive at that time and hence Ramanujan used to record only the result after solving the theorems on the slate.

During his time at Madras University, Ramanujan recorded his observations and deductions in four notebooks of loose-leaf paper. These four notebooks are still used as reference by mathematicians and scientists all around the world. The fourth of these notebooks, also called 'The Lost Notebook', was discovered only in 1976, in Cambridge, where he had spent nearly five years on the insistence of G.H. Hardy. Together, they formulated the Hardy–Ramanujan asymptotic formula, which is extensively used in physics. Ramanujan flourished as a scholar at Cambridge. Between 1916 and 1918, he was awarded a Bachelor of Arts by Research degree, was elected to the London Mathematical Society, and then appointed a Fellow of the Royal Society and a Fellow of Trinity College at Cambridge. He was only thirty-one at that time.

Growing up in extreme poverty led to many ailments, he had contracted smallpox, tuberculosis and other diseases. His health deteriorated further in England, which is why he returned to India in 1919. A year later, he died at the age of thirty-two. His birth anniversary on 22 December is celebrated as National Mathematics Day to honour the achievements of the legendary mathematician.

Ramanujan's mathematical achievements are still referred to in great depth even today. His short but spectacular life continues to influence areas of modern mathematics and physics 100 years since his death.

Google Boss

Name: Sundar Pichai
Birth Date: 10 June 1972
Place: Madurai, India

During the first round of his interview for the position of vice president in the product management department of Google, he was asked what he thought about Gmail. Google had announced the launch of their email service on that very day. Pichai hadn't seen Gmail yet and thought it could be an April Fools' Day joke.

By the third round of the interview, Pichai still had no answer to this question. In the fourth round, however, the interviewer asked him if he had seen Gmail and honest Pichai again replied in the negative. Though Pichai was well prepared for the interview, the question about Gmail was out of syllabus for him. He, however, showed his curiosity towards the product. To his surprise, the interviewer actually showed Gmail to him.

Therefore, he turned the moment of uncertainty into a learning opportunity and adapted brilliantly to the situation. When he could have pretended to know the answer, he showed intellectual humility in not knowing the answer and willingness to learn. After subsequent rounds of the interview, Pichai landed the job.

Sundar completed his schooling in Chennai, where he lived modestly with his family. He was known to have extraordinary memory where numbers were concerned. He graduated from IIT Kharagpur, then went to Stanford University and later to Wharton School in Pennsylvania. 'My dad and mom did what a lot of parents did at the time. They sacrificed a lot of their life and used a lot of their disposable income to make sure their children were educated,' he once said in an interview.

Before his glorious years at Google, he worked at McKinsey & Company for a short period of time. However, once he joined Google, there was no more change of jobs, rather progressive change of roles.

One of the projects that cemented his reputation at Google was Chrome, the web browser. What began as an experiment by his team of ten engineers is a popular search engine today. Since taking charge, he has overseen seven products, each of them used by more than a billion people: Search, YouTube, Gmail, Chrome, Maps, Android and the Google Play Store. Early in his career, he became instrumental in the release of Chromebook in 2009.

'We try to work on things which billions of people will use every day,' he is quoted saying.

In an interview at World Economic Forum, he stated how technology made an impact on him in the 1980s. He mentioned that back in India, when television was brought to his household, how discreetly it changed his life by giving him access to the rest of the world. In his own words, television for him was a 'first-hand experience of how gaining access to technology changes people's lives.' Sundar is an advocate of start-ups in India and believes, 'India will be a global player in the digital economy and it will be competitive with any country in the world . . . We are doing well as a country. We need to stay at it. We need a few more years and we will get to it. I am absolutely confident.'

As the CEO of Alphabet Inc., the parent company of Google, Pichai is heading the organization's efforts to advance machine learning and artificial intelligence that will make a difference in many fields.

A lot can be learnt from this quote of his: 'I do think it's important to follow your dreams and do something which you are excited by. If you follow your heart and do what you like, you will always do much better. It doesn't matter what your educational qualification is.'

Pichai showed the world that the son of a middle-class family in India could be one of the biggest success stories in the world of technology.

Maverick Poet

Name: Suryakant Tripathi 'Nirala'
Birth Date: 21 February 1896
Place: Midnapore, India
Death Date: 15 October 1961
Place: Prayagraj, India

This was in the mid-1950s. Pandit Jawaharlal Nehru, the Indian prime minister, had just returned from a trip to China. He was addressing a public meeting in his hometown, Prayagraj (then Allahabad). Nehru accepted a few garlands from his admirers before starting his speech. 'I have come from China,' he said, 'and there I heard a story of a great king who had two sons. One was considered wise, and the other foolish. When the boys reached adulthood, the king told the foolish one that he could have his throne, for he was fit only to be a ruler. But to the wise one, the ruler said that he was destined for far greater things—he would be a poet.'

In the audience, a bare-chested poet sat in the front row. The poet was also an avid wrestler and had come to listen to Pandit Nehru straight from the *akhara*. While his chest gleamed with oil befitting a wrestler, in contrast, his white beard and a streak of white hair on his head reflected the persona of a poet. However, his whole demeanour exuded a rebellious and liberated soul. All present in the pandal were surprised when Pandit Nehru finished his speech and flung his garlands at the poet's feet as an offering.

In the audience sat Nirala, the poet at whom Nehru had flung his garlands. Such was Nehru's admiration for him. Nehru further sanctioned a monthly allowance of Rs 100 for Nirala, realizing the great poet's financial strain.

Nirala was one of the greatest poets and essayists who infused his works with protest against social injustice and exploitation in society—a silent rebellion that literature is capable of exhibiting. The American novelist and translator David Rubin, who translated Nirala's works, says that in terms of genre, 'the range of Nirala's poetry is far greater than that of any other twentieth-century Hindi poet.'

Surprisingly, the great Hindi poet Nirala learnt Hindi much later in life. He had an interest in languages like Bengali and Sanskrit in early childhood. His wife, whom he had married at an early age, had inspired him to learn Hindi. However, tragedy struck when he lost his mother, wife and daughter in his early twenties.

After becoming proficient in Bengali, Sanskrit, English and Hindi, Nirala had a hard time finding a job. Due to a shortage of money, he accepted the job of a proofreader. What followed then was a path to becoming an editor and subsequently a writer.

Nirala always wrote from his heart. He was a fearless writer who wrote poems in Khari Boli (a dialect common in north Indian states), which led to a unique romantic movement in Hindi poetry.

Considered defiant where his writings were concerned, Nirala's works covered themes of love, nature, mysticism, nationalism and religion. He frequently questioned social and political beliefs in his writings. While the prose *Kulli Bhat* explores the caste system and homosexuality, the poem 'Saroj Smriti' describes his love and emotions towards his daughter. He introduced a new style of poetry with blank verse and freedom of form. According to David Rubin, the American novelist who translated Nirala's works to English, 'His (Niralas's) work was too startling in its originality, his satire too bitter, his break with the past too offensive to the orthodox, and the depth of his feeling either too troubling or too far beyond the common ken to assure wide popularity.' Perhaps this was what acquired him the pen name, 'Nirala' (meaning 'the strange one'/ 'the unique one').

Later in life, Nirala was diagnosed with schizophrenia and was admitted to the Central Institute of Psychiatry, Ranchi. The government of India issued a postage stamp in 1976 to honour this great poet of all time.

Woman of Substance

Name: Sushmita Sen
Birth Date: 19 November 1975
Place: Hyderabad, India

The day, 2 April 1984, marked a significant milestone in India's space journey as squadron leader Rakesh Sharma became the first Indian to be in space. When the then Prime Minister Indira Gandhi asked, 'How does India look from space?' he said, '*Saare jahan se achcha.*'

To millions of Indians who watched the telecast of this conversation, it was an emotional moment filled with pride. To many, it would serve as a source of inspiration to aspire to be the best in their chosen areas. But among the millions was a little girl, all of eight, who saw her baba, an air force officer, shedding tears of joy upon hearing Rakesh Sharma's reply.

It was a moment of reckoning for the little girl. She suddenly knew she wanted to be famous in life and wanted strangers to root for her, be mesmerized by her.

The girl grew up to be Sushmita Sen, the first Indian to win the Miss Universe title in 1994 and achieve global fame. She then acted in a number of Bollywood films.

However, her path to stardom was paved with great hard work and grit.

While other contestants at the Miss India pageant flaunted expensive outfits, Sushmita's gown was sewn by a local tailor. In an interview, she said, 'We bought a piece of fabric from Sarojini Nagar, a flea market in Delhi, and gave the material to the local tailor. Our only brief to him was—this will be shown on TV, make a good dress. He made my winning gown out of that fabric. We also bought brand new black socks, cut it, put elastic in it and then I wore them as gloves! You don't need money to get what you want, your intention should be right.'

Despite the financial limitations that didn't allow her to afford designer outfits, she had the confidence to walk the ramp in an unbranded gown at a pageant.

Not only did she inspire young girls to dream but she also bent many stereotypes associated with being a single parent, especially a mother. At twenty-four, she fought in court to adopt a girl and be a single parent.

Her strong will shone through the odds after doctors declared that she would be steroid-dependent for life due to adrenalin failure. Later her doctor said, 'In thirty-five years of my practice, somebody with an adrenalin failure has never come back to producing cortisol again.' Even after a slip disc, she went on to explore Aerial Silk—aerial acrobatics while hanging from a length of fabric. In the face of crisis, Sen only fought back.

She has been involved in social work and founded an NGO named the I AM Foundation, which aims to empower underprivileged children by giving them education and other welfare facilities.

Eight-year-old Sushmita may not have travelled to space, but she has touched the lives of so many young people, and inspired them to dream of the possibility of touching the stars.

The Cordon Bleu Chef

Name: Tarla Dalal
Birth Date: 3 June 1936
Place: Pune, India
Death Date: 6 November 2013
Place: Mumbai, India

Tarla married in 1960 and in those days, it was expected of the wife to take care of her husband's likes and dislikes—especially food. Her husband had always been keen on trying various dishes from world cuisine. Since Tarla was married into an affluent family, many household chores were taken care of and she had a lot of free time throughout the day. As a result, she decided to spend her time learning new dishes for her husband. Encouraged by her family, she joined a cooking school, where she learnt the art of exotic cooking.

Little did she know that while fulfilling her husband's wishes, she would garner worldwide popularity and be remembered for bringing the rest of the world to India—by expanding culinary horizons for Indians.

Every day at the school, Tarla would learn new dishes during the day and prepare them at home in the evenings for the family. Appreciation at home motivated her to study food. She started researching the science behind food and recorded recipes with exact quantities of ingredients. She always strove to create recipes with the least number of ingredients that were easy to work with and resulted in tasty food. Her cooking became popular in her circle of family and friends.

Consequently, a few friends urged her to start giving cooking lessons. The mushrooming popularity of the classes motivated her to write cookbooks so that the masses could benefit from the same. She released her first cookbook titled *Pleasures of Vegetarian Cooking* in 1974. It was just the start of a long string of cookbooks, which not only covered world cuisine but also successfully experimented with quick recipes, low-calorie food, scrumptious food for people with acidity, high blood pressure, diabetes, heart diseases, etc.—all of which were health compliant. Slowly, she was recognized as a prolific author and a nationwide icon among home cooks.

She revolutionized world cuisine by making it accessible for Indian consumers living in India in the 1960s and onwards. Her recipes were tailor-made for an Indian kitchen—temperatures in Celsius, measurements in teacups and ingredient lists suitable for local grocery stores. Her recipes covered a wide variety, from aloo paratha to salads with dressings to Chinese fried rice and Italian dishes like lasagne and risotto, as well as ice cream and miscellaneous desserts such as apple pie, chocolate soufflé and many more.

By the late 1980s, her books had become so famous that they were translated into several Indian and international languages. Celebrated chef Sanjeev Kapoor said, 'Her books made it possible for many millions of people to know about international food in a very affordable and accessible way.'

Quickly embracing technology and believing in moving ahead with the times, she launched her website as early as 1988. It was the most visited cookery website in those days. Her YouTube channel has videos of hundreds of recipes.

Tarla believed in simple, quick, reproducible and economical food. 'You see, good cooking is not difficult technically, with some guidance and encouragement, any person with a liking for food, interest in cooking and a little patience can, instead of being just an ordinary cook, become an excellent one.'

Awarded the Padma Shri in 2007 for her contributions to cooking, Tarla Dalal left a legacy that transcended geography, gender and class.

The Master Chef

Name: Vikas Khanna
Birth Date: 14 November 1971
Place: Amritsar, India

Growing up, Vikas had an uneven gait. His arms and legs were misaligned at birth, which meant he had to wear special heavy wooden shoes that did help him walk, but made him look 'awkward' as he lumbered along with some effort. More than the physical discomfort, Vikas was scarred by kids making fun of his condition. To avoid them, Vikas would sneak into the kitchen, which became his refuge.

Watching his biji cook, Vikas slowly found his interest in cooking deepen. He meticulously observed the variety and quantity of spices his grandmother used. Seated on a stool, he started asking questions about spices and their combinations, which his grandmother answered in great detail.

A mobility limitation helped Vikas discover his true passion in life—cooking. At fifteen, with the help of his mother, Vikas overcame that limitation. She took him to a park, removed his wooden shoes and asked him to run. While his legs felt weak, he ran. And he left his disability behind.

Since then, there has been no looking back for Vikas.

In his late teens, he opened his own catering business, through which he learnt important lessons about hospitality, customer service and how to value a customer above everything else. While his family encouraged him to become an engineer, Vikas was cut out for bigger dreams in life. Chasing his interest in cooking, he graduated in hotel management, after which he joined the Leela Group and subsequently, the Taj Group of Hotels, even doing a short stint at Welcomgroup. Later, he went to pursue a professional course at New York University.

He shone on the global stage and gained worldwide acclaim, which culminated in his restaurant, Junoon, being awarded a Michelin star—a review rating for restaurants all around the world—for six consecutive years. Receiving a Michelin star is to restaurants what receiving an Oscar is to movies!

He has represented India on many international platforms, including the uber-popular TV show, MasterChef Australia, as a guest judge. Cooking for the Obamas, the Dalai Lama and a seven-course meal for Narendra Modi and top CEOs when the Indian PM was visiting the US are some of his biggest achievements. He has written not only cookbooks but also storybooks for children too. His books *The Milk Moustache* and *The Magic Rolling Pin* are enjoyed greatly by kids.

Vikas emulates philanthropy, which perhaps is reminiscent of his childhood memories of a langar in Amritsar. During the Covid-19 lockdown, his Feed India initiative went on to become one of the largest food drives, and served millions of meals. He is also involved with projects that aid victims of natural disasters, such as tsunamis, floods, landslides among others.

Today, Vikas Khanna is recognized as one of the most iconic chefs of the world. He charmed diners globally with Indian cooking. He is also instrumental in the setting up of the Museum of Culinary Arts in Manipal, to preserve and showcase India's rich culinary heritage. The simplicity and love for his roots are infused in his cooking. Perhaps, it was a result of spending his formative years with his biji in the kitchen.

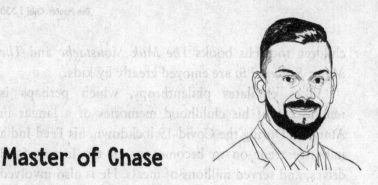

Master of Chase

Name: Virat Kohli
Birth Date: 5 November 1988
Place: New Delhi, India

Eighteen-year-old Virat was playing in his debut Ranji season and was the overnight batsman for Delhi, batting at 40 not out against Karnataka. With an ongoing season, in the early hours of 18 December 2006, he lost his father, who was battling a cerebral stroke. While the atmosphere in the house was sombre, Virat did not shed a tear. Though he could take the day off, somewhere deep within, a voice told him that not going to a cricket match was never an option. Virat had a quick word with his coach and showed up for the game. Delhi was precariously perched at 103/5 when Virat walked in and went on to score 90, saving the day for his team.

After the match in the evening, he returned home and joined the family for his father's cremation. That day, Virat promised his brother that he would go on to play the game for his country. On arguably the saddest day of his life, he derived immense mental fortitude to play his best and honour the vision of his father, who had wanted Virat to play at the highest level. While success did not immediately knock on his door after his father's death, Virat continued to march forward steadily.

Today, he is regarded as one of the best contemporary cricketers to have played the game, both as a swashbuckling batsman and a successful captain.

Hero-worshipping Sachin Tendulkar, like thousands of other Indian kids who played cricket in the congested lanes of their localities, Virat also wanted to become a cricketer. His father, Prem Kohli, noticed extraordinary keenness in his son to learn cricket and admitted nine-year-old Virat to the West Delhi Cricket Academy in 1998. Initially, nobody saw anything exceptional in his game. However, a few days later, what caught everyone's attention was neither his batting nor bowling, but the speed with which he threw the ball back while fielding.

Favouritism and nepotism were prevalent in selection committees in those days. According to Kohli, during his early playing days, his father refused to give a bribe that could have confirmed him a spot in Delhi's state team. His father made it clear that Virat must get a spot on his own merit or not at all. In an interview, Virat said, 'I was broken but that showed me that the world works like this. If you need to go ahead, do things that no one else is doing. So that was the lesson he gave me and I saw that from my father who made a life for himself and gave me the right teachings by actions.'

Virat practised diligently, he listened to his coaches, corrected his mistakes and showed phenomenal progress in his game. Eventually, the selectors started noticing him. He always delivered even under pressure. His big moment arrived at the age of fourteen, when he received the 'Player of the Tournament' award at a school-level tournament. After that, there was no looking back. He played innumerable national and international matches. He went on to break Sachin Tendulkar's record of scoring the fastest 10,000 runs in one-day internationals in 2018.

Today, along with his partner, Anushka Sharma, Virat also works for the Virat Kohli Foundation, which supports underprivileged aspiring athletes in any sport by connecting them to resources. Not only this, but the foundation is also working towards saving stray animals.

He has been granted many national and international awards, including the Padma Shri (2017), Rajiv Gandhi Khel Ratna (2018), Sir Garfield Sobers Award for ICC Male Cricketer of the Decade (2011–2020) and ICC Cricketer of the Year (2017).

Virat Kohli completely changed the landscape of modern cricket and introduced a unique fitness culture to the sport, which makes him a player who is in a league of his own. At a young age, Virat has garnered greatness in cricket and cricket fans across the globe continue to marvel at the unreal skills he displays on the field. He believes, 'Whatever you want to do, do with full passion and work hard towards it. Do not look anywhere else. There will be a few distractions, but if you can be true to yourself, you will be successful.'

Conductor of Melodies

Name: Zubin Mehta
Birth Date: 29 April 1936
Place: Mumbai, India

Being born to a musician father, music was a family legacy to Zubin Mehta. It is even said that he started speaking and singing at the same time. At two, after receiving a pair of drumsticks, Zubin used them ceaselessly on household objects to produce 'music'. When the family took away the drumsticks to ensure the safety of their household items, little Zubin caught hold of spoons from the kitchen and resumed his attack.

Unlike most children at that age, who are usually engrossed in toys, Zubin's attention was claimed entirely by musical instruments. Even before he learnt how to read, Zubin could identify his favourite records by the colour of the label and would ask the nanny to play them on the gramophone at home. While still a child, he would often 'pretend' to be a conductor.

Music was so deeply integral to him at an early age that when he fell sick, he would stop crying when his much-loved records were played and resume crying as soon as the music ended. Even while cycling or playing cricket, Zubin could be heard whistling beautifully. He grew up in a musical environment, about which he spoke in one of his interviews, 'I grew up in these surroundings with my father practising music in the living room, and with the musical scores scattered all around the house. I liked looking at them even though I could barely read them. My father also had something marvellous, a record player on which we could listen to music endlessly.'

Zubin inherited a passion for Western classical music from his father.

He was born in 1936 to Tehmina Mehta and Mehli Mehta in Mumbai. His father, who was also a concert violinist, was his first music teacher. He taught Zubin to play the violin and piano. By the time he was in his teens, the young musician was conducting the full orchestra during rehearsals of the Mumbai Symphony Orchestra, which his father helped found in 1935.

As he grew up around music, his mother was concerned and wanted him to make a career in a 'respectable' profession. Therefore, though not happily, he studied medicine. But after two years of medical studies, he convinced his family that he only wanted a career in music. His family supported his passion and sent him to study music at the University of Music and Performing Arts Vienna in 1954.

Zubin took admission in a conducting programme under Hans Swarowsky at the Akademie für Musik. In 1956, he organized a student orchestra to conduct a concert at a refugee camp outside Vienna in only seven days. Only a genius could achieve this. His first professional milestone was in 1958 when he won the Liverpool International Conducting Competition. He was just twenty-two at the time.

By 1961, he had already conducted the Vienna, Berlin and Israel Philharmonic Orchestras. His hard work, dedication and success led him to become the music director of many orchestras, including the Montreal Symphony Orchestra, the Los Angeles Philharmonic, the Israel Philharmonic Orchestra, the New York Philharmonic and the Maggio Musicale Fiorentino.

Zubin sees a bigger role for music beyond personal gratification; for him, music also has a public purpose—a tool to protest as well as something that can make people think. Hence, he has never shied away from holding concerts in politically sensitive areas or from taking political stands. For example, he refused to perform in South Africa several times due to apartheid and conducted a concert in Kashmir in 2013 to stand in solidarity with the citizens.

Zubin has conducted orchestras for the last sixty years all over the world. In one of his interviews with Luke Slattery, the maestro said, 'When I started leading the Vienna Philharmonic, I was conducting my professors. Later, when I returned, I was conducting my colleagues from the school. Now they've all retired and I'm conducting young kids I don't know. But the tradition is carrying on.'

Regarded as one of the twentieth century's greatest conductors, Zubin Mehta, by his admission, entered this musical pleasure garden as a very young person and so far, nothing and no one have managed to drive him away from it.

READ MORE IN PUFFIN

The Puffin Book of 100 Great Indians

 Now with an exciting new cover, *The Puffin Book of 100 Great Indians* is a celebration of achievements and personal stories of those who forged new paths for themselves and others in a way that it continues to affect modern lives.

Written as short anecdotal biographical sketches, this book presents lives of scientists, doctors, activists, painters, sportspeople, dancers, political leaders, economists and many more from different walks of life.

Featured in this collection are pioneering mathematician Aryabhata, missile man Dr Kalam, economist and Nobel laureate Dr Amartya Sen, India's Renaissance man Raja Ram Mohan Roy, the immortal star in space Kalpana Chawla, master blaster Sachin Tendulkar, the evergreen melody queen Lata Mangeshkar—some of the great luminaries who have made incredible contributions in diverse fields.